WITTGENSTEIN AND KIERKEGAARD

CHARLES L. CREEGAN

WITTGENSTEIN AND KIERKEGAARD

Religion, individuality, and philosophical method

CHARLES L. CREEGAN

ROUTLEDGE

LONDON AND NEW YORK

First published in 1989 by Routledge
11 New Fetter Lane, London EC4P 4EE
29 West 35th Street, New York, NY 10001

© 1989 Charles L. Creegan

Printed in Great Britain
by TJ Press (Padstow) Ltd
Padstow, Cornwall

All rights reserved. No part of this book may be reprinted or reproduced or utilized in any form or by any electronic, mechanical, or other means, now known or hereafter invented, including photocopying and recording, or in any information storage or retrieval system, without permission in writing from the publishers.

British Library Cataloguing in Publication Data

Creegan, Charles L. 1959–
Wittgenstein and Kierkegaard: religion, individuality and philosophical method.
1. English philosophy. Wittgenstein, Ludwig, 1889–1951 2. Danish philosophy. Kierkegaard, Søren, 1813–1855
I. Title
192

ISBN 0-415-00066-1

Library of Congress Cataloging in Publication Data

Creegan, Charles L., 1959–
Wittgenstein and Kierkegaard : religion, individuality, and philosophical method / Charles L. Creegan.
p. cm.
Bibliography: p.
Includes index.
ISBN 0-415-00066-1
1. Wittgenstein, Ludwig, 1889–1951—Contributions in methodology. 2. Wittgenstein, Ludwig, 1889–1951—Religion. 3. Wittgenstein, Ludwig, 1889–1951—Contributions in individuality. 4. Kierkegaard, Søren, 1813–1855—Influence. 5. Kierkegaard, Søren, 1813–1855—Contribution in methodology. 6. Kierkegaard, Søren, 1813–1855—Contribution in individuality. 7. Religion—Philosophy. 8. Methodology. 9. Individuality. I. Title.
B3376.W564C74 1989
192—dc19

88 23633

CONTENTS

	Introduction	1
1	RELEVANT BIOGRAPHY	8
2	METHODOLOGY	30
3	PROBLEMS OF INTERPRETATION	52
4	IMPLICATIONS FOR RELIGION	73
5	ECHOES AND REPERCUSSIONS	97
6	NOW I CAN GO ON!	119
	Notes	124
	Bibliography	143
	Index	152

INTRODUCTION

The works of Søren Kierkegaard and Ludwig Wittgenstein are generally conceded to be of seminal importance for their respective fields. But the mention of 'respective fields' already shows that there is a radical gap between the spheres of influence of the two authors.

A systematic consideration of the situation could result in a variety of theories concerning the origin of this gap. For example, it might seem to be justified by the disparity in the two authors' own fields of study. Kierkegaard explicitly claims to be 'a religious author,' insisting that everything he writes must be understood in relation to the problem of 'becoming a Christian.' On the other hand, Wittgenstein is clearly a philosopher: in his works the problems of philosophy are addressed in terms of the relation between language and world. These facts certainly document a substantial difference.

The impression that Kierkegaard and Wittgenstein are not participants in the same universe of discourse might be further substantiated by the fundamental difference in their motivations. Kierkegaard felt a vocation of religious edification, which he discovered and expressed through his relations with other people, his father, fiancée, and bishop being chief among these. His appeal to the categories of philosophy derives from his psychological perception of the religious 'need of the age.' Wittgenstein came to philosophy through its connection with fields far removed from religion. He began as an engineer, and engaged certain technical questions in the philosophy of mathematics and logic as a natural outgrowth of this interest. Eventually his investigations into symbolism led to a more general interest in language; the language of religion is only one of the examples he considered. Once again, there is a considerable difference to be seen.

These differences between Kierkegaard and Wittgenstein help to explain the appropriation of Kierkegaard by 'Continental' existentialists and theologians, and the appeals to Wittgenstein by 'Anglo-American' logical positivists, analytic philosophers, and philosophers of language.

The separation between readers of Wittgenstein and Kierkegaard has become even wider as a result of the logical positivists' well-known antipathy toward religion. The association of Wittgenstein with their position, despite his disavowals, has virtually ensured the propagation in the scholarly world of the impression that he not only ignored religion but positively abhorred it. Thus 'Wittgensteinian' philosophers might be inclined to disregard Kierkegaard, while some theologians and scholars of religion display actual fear of Wittgenstein.[1]

The difference between the two authors can be briefly summarized as follows: Kierkegaard is 'the father of existentialism,' while Wittgenstein is 'the father of analytic philosophy.' What greater difference could there be?

In the midst of their legitimate differences, there is one similarity between Kierkegaard and Wittgenstein which is striking. This similarity cannot be expressed in systematic categories: it is not a case of identity in academic specialization, nor yet of correlation in factual discoveries. Instead, it is a congruity of *method*. Both authors stress reliance on indirect methods of communication; both rely on such methods themselves.

The term 'indirect communication' was coined by Kierkegaard. Wittgenstein's parallel concept, which carries over from the early to the later period, is the 'showing' of certain essential ideas or distinctions which cannot be 'said.' Both methods are based on the perspicuous presentation of evidence, rather than the advancing of 'theses,' concerning the various subjects under consideration.

Since both authors are communicating indirectly, it is not surprising that some of the strategies of communication they use are the same. Certain features are repeatedly evident in their works. Among these are examples, reminders, repetition of the obvious, notes on usage, and stories.

These elements are used in a unique way. They are not

presented as factually significant 'data.' Rather, they are proposed as clues to the solutions of certain problems, and to the grasping of usage within the conceptual schemes of which their original application forms a part.

Once this parallel in methodology is recognized, it quickly becomes clear that there is a variety of important connections between the two authors. Neither adopted 'indirect communication' as a matter of chance. Rather, this strategy arose from the nature of their particular concerns.

Kierkegaard and Wittgenstein agree that there are areas in which dialectical thought is simply incompetent. But neither author is content to accept the limits of reasoned discussion as ultimate. The particular problems which both address are in areas which have always had uncertain but important relations with reason: religion and the traditional 'metaphysical' realm. Both mark out the delineation (and not primarily the examination) of these areas as their special province.

The use of new methods by both Wittgenstein and Kierkegaard is closely related to their interest in religion and metaphysical problems. One feature of much philosophizing which both authors believe to be problematic is the effort to use the wrong tools, that is, to carry through the techniques of reason to these foundational areas. They agree that the use of systematic categories in an attempt to 'understand everything' has led a drift away from fruitful thinking. Because metaphysics and religion *are* foundational, this drift gains considerable leverage in philosophy and everyday life.

Both authors propose to apply an influence which will serve as a 'corrective' to the systematic drift. In order to counteract the existing leverage, their influence may need to take a radical form. But it is important to distinguish this radical therapy from a radical position. Wittgenstein and Kierkegaard agree that they can do no better than to explicate what is already the case.

Both contend that the explication which they attempt gets further than reasoned explanation does; they also agree that nevertheless it too must 'stop somewhere.' But neither believes that where he has stopped in his commentary is 'the end.' Both are interested in transitions and activities which can only start *after* the philosophical discussion is over. Problems may have been eliminated, or at least clarified; but little has been settled. Yet to have shown how little is settled when these problems are solved is itself an important achievement.

The question of method takes on added importance in view of the authors' refusal to come to systematic conclusions. There is little distinction to be made between the construction of their work and its final results. Many strategies are both used and recommended, often at the same time. A remark may be germane to more than one discussion. Both authors make a conscious effort to employ a suggestive, rather than a reductive method. They prefer to expand discourse rather than to limit it.

The refusal to be systematic has one root in the indirect method and the difficulties of expression that prompted its adoption. But the connection between the method used and that explicated is also connected with the personal dimension of the two authors' work. They were bound up in their problems. Kierkegaard spoke of his authorship as a 'task'; he often agonized over the decision to publish a book. Wittgenstein's philosophical struggles were evident in his classes. He rethought each problem as he spoke of it. The integration of life and works is a feature which each author understood and cultivated. Their lives are important reminders in the showing of their purposes.

Readers of the two authors' works are not spared the personal involvement which the authors themselves felt. Indirect communication demands that the 'task' of philosophy falls at least as much on the shoulders of the audience as on those of the speaker. Both Kierkegaard and Wittgenstein hoped that their work might have uses in the daily life of their audiences.

Most studies take on some of the flavor of the works under review. But in light of the fact that both Kierkegaard and Wittgenstein look to their readers to continue in the appropriate way, any work 'about' them must adhere to their categories more closely than usual – must in fact become work 'with' or 'after' them. Three ideas about method, held in common by the two figures, will be constantly adopted in this particular investigation.

The first recommendation to be appropriated is that of limitation of the task. Kierkegaard's work was expressly limited. He was constantly concerned with one problem: that of 'becoming a Christian.'[2] Wittgenstein too always had a 'particular purpose' in mind;[3] once a specific problem was solved, suggestions for general

INTRODUCTION

(systematic?) improvements were met with the imperative: 'Leave the *bloody* thing *alone!*'[4] So while it would doubtless be possible to fill an encyclopedia with the catalogue of differences between Kierkegaard and Wittgenstein, it would hardly be in their spirit to make the attempt.

The suggestion of an unrecognized parallel between Kierkegaard and Wittgenstein brings this study into another of their categories, the 'corrective.' The many differences between the two authors are generally obvious, like the religious/not religious dichotomy, and are not likely to be forgotten. As a corrective, this work will often be concerned with recalling well-known facts about the two authors which *have* been forgotten.

The investigation of these similarities will require the use of another component of the method recommended by the two authors – stressing certain parts of their work in a new pattern, and thus altering the flavor of the synthetic understanding, much like Kierkegaard's 'dash of cinnamon.'[5] Such a project will be concerned to 'assemble reminders' suggestive of the new stress.[6] As a result of this change in stress, some 'obvious facts' may be thrown into question.

In order to bring the parallels between Kierkegaard and Wittgenstein out most fully, the above-mentioned tools must be applied to several different areas.

In light of the fact that both authors felt close connections between life and authorship, the first part of the 'task' must be to establish more closely the extent of parallels between the styles of their lives.

The results of this investigation can be one guide to a better grasp of the methods which they used and set forth in their works. Certainly such a grasp is necessary if the aim of these methods is ever to be clarified.

Against the background of both life and method, some previous attempts to 'understand' the positions they took on the key subject of the individual will be examined. In making this examination, it will be important to remember the close relations each author felt between his own individuality and his work, and their refusals to be systematic in their investigations and categories.

With this example of the application and results of their method in mind, some implications for the field of religion (in which both had a personal interest) can be laid out. This examination will begin from the systematic categorization of Kierkegaard as religious and Wittgenstein as non-religious.

Finally, the possibility of further work in the tradition of Kierkegaard and Wittgenstein will be explored. By this time it will be obvious that such a continuation could not be carried out in the modes usually associated with philosophy.

No comparative and corrective endeavor can be perfectly symmetrical. Different thinkers and different extrapolations by varying communities of interpretation will naturally suggest the need for varying reminders. In the particular cases of Kierkegaard and Wittgenstein, difficulties are raised by the different aims embodied in the two authorships. Kierkegaard was primarily concerned to communicate. He had a sense of urgency concerning the specific existential problem of finitude and its possible working out in faith. In the course of this communication he used certain tools. Wittgenstein spent more time at the reflexive or recursive task of communicating about communication, and investigating investigation. In the course of this project he worked on some problems essential to the method, and tested his tools on various other problems. Thus, in order to grasp the direction of his approach, relatively more synoptic presentation of his tactics may be needed. Kierkegaard's fixed goal simplifies the investigation of his methodology; and his methods may serve as examples of the kind of solutions which Wittgenstein recommended and tried to use.

In the investigation of the relevance of Wittgenstein's thought for religion the same problem will occur. Kierkegaard's interest in religion is well known, and given this clue its influence can be ferreted out even where it is not obvious. But even the possibility of applying Wittgenstein's categories to religion in a non-destructive way may have to be demonstrated; clues must be sought before they can be used. To show that he himself might have made such applications is yet another problem.

But irrespective of the relative amounts of reconsideration, this study depends on a mutual relation of suggestiveness. Both in the wider problem of method and the specific problem of faith, the terms which Kierkegaard employed (such as 'without authority' and 'the individual') often clarify a dimension in Wittgenstein's life and work. Wittgenstein's categories (such as 'form of life' and 'showing') give new reach and grounding to Kierkegaard's project.

INTRODUCTION

That two authors with such divergent motivations might come to make such similar recommendations at key points suggests that their new methodology has broader implications than have yet been realized. In the final analysis, even their irreconcilable differences make the similarities between them more important.

Chapter One

RELEVANT BIOGRAPHY

The 'particular purpose' of this chapter and the next is to come to an understanding of each author's method and goals. Four different kinds of material must be combed for 'reminders' germane to this task: biographical or autobiographical sources, and passages from philosophical works which reveal biographical events (intentionally or otherwise); the structure of philosophical works, and direct statements in these works. The first two, more 'biographical' kinds of evidence will be dealt with in this chapter; the second two, more 'philosophical' kinds must wait until the next chapter.

An important subsection of the biographical task is to show (so far as possible) the extent of Kierkegaard's direct influence on Wittgenstein. Only a very few explicit references to Kierkegaard exist in works by Wittgenstein, or memoirs of him. But it is easy to see that this is one of the many cases in which Wittgenstein was influenced by other thinkers in an amount far out of proportion to the number of explicit references in his works and notebooks.

WITTGENSTEIN

The texture of Wittgenstein's life is itself an important clue to understanding his work. He did not lead an organized and settled existence, even by the standards of his time, which was interrupted by two wars. Most of his life was episodic in character. This was true even of his relatively settled Cambridge academic periods. It is surely not a coincidence that his philosophy is episodic and aphoristic. Both his life and philosophy mirror the incredible breadth of his interests, as well as the nervousness of his character.

The path by which he first arrived at Cambridge is an excellent example. His interest in aeronautics led him from the *Technische Hochschule* at Berlin-Charlottenburg to England. He enrolled as a research student at the University of Manchester in 1908. There he pursued in rapid succession interests in kite-flying, airplane motors, propellers, then the mathematics of propellers, the foundations of mathematics, and mathematical logic – all of which led him to a meeting with Bertrand Russell in October 1911.[1] He studied with Russell from then until the outbreak of the First World War. This rapid succession of interests, each of which he was competent to pursue (even though they are connected only by the most tenuous of 'family resemblances'), is characteristic of Wittgenstein's life.

It is inevitable that the reports of Wittgenstein's life are also fragmentary. Even information about his most settled periods in Cambridge exists only in an anecdotal form. Various students and colleagues have recorded their impressions. But to date there has not even been a synthetic study taking all of the available material into account, let alone any attempt to tackle the task (by now impossible) of filling in the gaps in this material. These gaps are partly a product of his intensely private nature. His dislike of publicity was sensed by many of his colleagues; although they knew that he was an important figure, they felt it would be a violation of his wishes to keep notes about him.

Three foci are clear in the mosaic of impressions. One is Wittgenstein's dissatisfaction with the gap between his moral ideals and his ability to fulfill them. This is repeatedly evident. A second is his understanding of the nature of philosophy. His own ideas of how to philosophize, and his disdain for academic 'philosophy,' help to make this attitude clear. The third, which itself links the previous two, is his understanding of the close connections between ethical, aesthetic, moral, and philosophical concerns. Again, this trait is demonstrated in the perfection he demanded in life, in philosophy, and even in the house he constructed.

These three features are all more or less evident in various episodes from Wittgenstein's life. To grasp fully the significance of the whole, it is necessary to follow a method which he suggested in the 'Lecture on Ethics':

> I will put before you a number of more or less synonymous expressions ... and by enumerating them I want to produce the

same sort of effect which Galton produced when he took a number of photos of different faces on the same photographic plate ... so if you look through the row of synonyms which I will put before you, you will, I hope, be able to see the characteristic features they all have in common.²

In the following material, some of the synthetic work has been done; but the most important episodes are presented whole.

One feature of Wittgenstein's self-understanding was his exaggerated sense of his moral imperfection, even worthlessness. As his letters show, his hope for self-improvement varied, so that he was at times more or less cheerfully resigned, and at times positively suicidal.³ This self-image was not lightly arrived at. The high level of his standards is illustrated by a term of approbation he used: 'He is a *human being!*'⁴ Wittgenstein often felt that he himself failed to live up to this high basic standard. He was sometimes criticized for undue harshness toward others; but as his letters attest, his harshness was equally directed toward himself. This trait influenced the way in which he did philosophy; it may have been responsible for the fact that he did not publish the *Investigations* during his lifetime, although the manuscript of Part One was in more or less its final form for several years before his death. In a letter to Malcolm, he says: 'it's pretty lousy. (Not that I could improve on it essentially if I tried for another 100 years.)'⁵

The *Investigations* is only a small part of Wittgenstein's *Nachlaß*. Malcolm reports that between 1929 and 1951 he produced roughly 30,000 pages of philosophical material, in notebooks, manuscripts, and typescripts.⁶ The sheer amount of this material provides an important insight into Wittgenstein's way of thinking. Both the *Tractatus* and the *Investigations* began as material collected in notebooks, in which the same general line of thought was often explored several times in slightly different ways. Preliminary attempts at a more definitive collection followed. (These are published as the *Protractatus* and the *Brown Book*.) The final material was carefully selected and polished, down to the last individual word choice.

The pains taken in preparing written material were made visible (literally) in Wittgenstein's classroom style. He offered 'lectures' which resembled Platonic dialogues, with Wittgenstein taking the part of Socrates and his students that of the overawed foils. A group of college students he once visited exclaimed that they had 'never *seen* a man thinking before.'[7] And this idea is echoed by many of his biographers: even if the ground was familiar to him, he attacked it each time freshly; he 'did philosophy' in each class.

One of Wittgenstein's characteristic philosophical tools was the use of outlandish examples to illuminate everyday life. At the same time, he often noticed problems in other philosophers' apparently more mundane metaphors. His sister Hermine helps to explain this great ability to discriminate between good and bad examples. She reports that the Wittgenstein children often communicated in comparisons. For example, she once suggested that his decision to teach in rural schools was like wanting to use a precision instrument to open crates. He replied that others were seeing the gyrations of his life as through a closed window – not realizing that he was struggling to keep his feet in a hurricane.[8] The inventiveness learned in this kind of communication clearly carried over to Ludwig's philosophizing.

The active nature of Wittgenstein's philosophical work made it physically and emotionally demanding. After a lecture he would often go to a movie. He preferred American westerns, films that were undemanding and escapist. He sat in the front row, filling his visual field with the screen. And while he paid very close attention, sitting on the edge of his seat, and demanding quiet from his companions (as Malcolm reports), he was cleansed and relaxed by the experience. 'This is like a shower bath!' he once exclaimed.[9]

Wittgenstein's penchant for *active* philosophizing also helps to account for the fact that he was not very well read in the history of philosophy. He once assured a student that 'no assistant lecturer in philosophy in the country had read fewer books on philosophy than he had.'[10] He read a great deal of Plato, but no Aristotle at all! Most of his favorite authors were suggestive and moral, rather than rigorous and logical, in their writings; in addition to Kierkegaard, Saint Augustine, Dostoevsky, and Tolstoy are often mentioned. It was Tolstoy's abridgement of the Gospels that he discovered during the First World War, and carried with him. He read George Fox with approbation. Schopenhauer's *World as Will and Idea* was one of his earliest philosophical readings. He read, and was excited by, William James's *Varieties of Religious Experience* as early as 1912. He believed that it caused a moral improvement in him.[11]

The paucity of Wittgenstein's philosophical reading was a

conscious decision. It should not be taken as a sign of general lack of culture; in fact, he was formidably cultured, as can be seen in many of the examples used in his works. His talents in music were considerable. When he was a schoolteacher, he was required to play a musical instrument. He selected the clarinet. He was also a virtuoso whistler, and displayed a conductor's memory and understanding of orchestral pieces.

Another reason why Wittgenstein read little philosophy was that he disdained academia-for-its-own-sake. 'Professorial philosophy by philosophy professors,' or non-genuine philosophizing, was one of Wittgenstein's greatest dislikes.[12] He often tried to discourage his best students from becoming professors. Several of them report that he seems to have been afraid they would cheat their students – and themselves – by offering a course in philosophy. (He seemed to believe that no one could deliver what 'philosophy' promises.[13]) He suggested that instead they should do useful work. This fits, not only with his remarks on philosophy in general, but with his expressions of his own inadequacy as a teacher. He was sure that his teaching had done more harm than good to his students. He twice left the academic scene because he felt he had nothing more to contribute, and there is evidence that he had considered leaving more often.

Wittgenstein's moral stiffness was evident in his conduct of his own life, as well as in his advice to his students. The family fortune was quite large; through good management it survived the First World War and the post-war depression. But upon his return from the war, he insisted on deeding his share to his brothers and sisters. Hermine Wittgenstein recalls that he wore out the notary with his repeated demands that there must be no way in which he could ever claim the money again! But she also reports that he would never worry about asking for help from them when in need – so he would always survive, like Alyusha Karamazov.[14] If this is true, he was not nearly so forthright about borrowing money from his friends. He was constantly concerned that he might be a burden to them, as his letters show. He never hesitated to lend, if he could.

Along with the giving up of his claim to fortune came a general simplification of his lifestyle. When he was at Manchester, he dressed stylishly;[15] but he came to be famous for his unostentatious dress: an open-necked shirt (never a tie), wool overshirt or windbreaker, more rarely a topcoat, and sometimes a cloth cap.

His eating habits, too, were simple. He was quite content to eat the same ordinary fare meal after meal, even on occasion preferring such food to more elaborate meals specially prepared. This seems to have been a conscious ethical/aesthetic choice for simplicity. Complexity was allowed, and energy was expended, only where necessary, in important matters. Unnecessary energy and complexity could only be distractions.

While at Cambridge, Wittgenstein did not dine at high table – the conversation sickened him. The sparseness of his various rooms is famous. There was in general only a cot, a table for writing, and a few books; extra chairs were piled on the landing for use during classes. He lived in an equally frugal manner during his vacations (in rural parts of Norway and Ireland), and during his schoolteaching days.

Wittgenstein's sense of his moral duty showed itself very strongly in his service during the two World Wars. If his status as a member of a rich industrial family had not been enough to excuse him from active duty during the first war, he could also have claimed a medical exemption, for he had had a double hernia. But he insisted on enlisting. Nor was he content with the rear echelon duties that he was given; his continual attempts to get to the front were finally rewarded when he was trained as an artillery officer. He respected Russell's pacifist stand; yet he thought that such a position would not be right for him.

It is very interesting to note that at least some of the final work on the *Tractatus* was done while he was at the front. He did not find his military duty disagreeable, even though he was serving in a tough mountain campaign.[16]

During the Second World War Wittgenstein served as a laboratory technician, first in a hospital dispensary, and later in a research facility. The quality of his work was appreciated in both places. Whatever his occupation, Wittgenstein undertook to do as well as possible.

The reasons for Wittgenstein's decision to become a rural schoolteacher are much disputed. His sister Hermine reports that she herself found it hard to understand, and he explained it with the metaphor of the hurricane. This suggests a morally based decision, perhaps a desire actually to earn his living and to 'serve' as he could not in 'philosophy.' The idea that his decision had to do with his moral self-understanding is supported by the fact that he spent some time as a gardener at a monastery before taking up his teaching duties.

Wittgenstein spent several years at three different schools in rural Lower Austria. He had better than average success in the classroom. But his eccentricity and uncompromising nature, as well as the project of school reform which his presence symbolized, did not endear him to the parents of his students. According to Bartley, Wittgenstein was even tried (on dubious grounds) at one posting; though acquitted, he decided to give up teaching.[17] Afterwards he again spent a few months as a gardener at a second monastery.

The most enduring expression of Wittgenstein's moral nature is the house which he and Paul Engelmann built for Margarete Stonborough. Assessments of the respective contributions of the two men to the project vary widely. As the house is very much in the style of Adolf Loos, it might be impossible to determine the boundaries between common interest and influence. Both of them had known Loos as early as 1914. Engelmann was Loos's student; Wittgenstein met Loos through an introduction from the publisher Ficker, and Wittgenstein actually met Engelmann through an introduction from Loos. The three men were in substantial agreement about the principles of architecture, as Engelmann makes clear in his memoir.[18] Unfortunately, the portion of the memoir which would have covered the period of the construction of the house was never written.

There can be no doubt that the uncompromising nature of the house as built suits Wittgenstein very well. It is uncompromising both in its plainness and in the attention to detail which emphasizes this plainness. No one disputes that Wittgenstein had a lot to do with the execution of technical details.

The plainness of the house is backed by a mathematical rigor in the design, which again suggests Wittgenstein at work. On the main floor, the size and placement of doors is in strict ratio to the dimensions of the walls. The rooms themselves are exactly proportioned in simple ratios. The geometrical calculations were carefully done, and Wittgenstein went so far as to have finished work torn out in order to correct fractional deviations from the plan. This strictness, combined with the lack of frills, might be expected to impart considerable severity to the house, but instead it is very airy and pleasant. Hermine Wittgenstein refers to it as a '*hausgewordene Logik*'; but its logic is the logic of a dwelling. She also reports that it suited the grand and peculiar nature of her sister Margarete very well.[19] Pictures and drawings of the house as furnished show a variety of unusual objects which are set off by the plainness of the background.

Bernhard Leitner suggests that Wittgenstein was an architect by virtue of (and not in addition to) his being a philosopher.[20] The connection between ethics, aesthetics, and logic expressed in the *Tractatus* is made manifest in the house.

One further kind of anecdote will illustrate Wittgenstein's sense of moral duty. On at least two occasions in the 1940s, he had the opportunity to get a substantial amount of money through 'philosophy.' He was asked to give the John Locke lectures at Oxford for a fee of £200; he refused because he could not imagine the lectures being any good. Again, Malcolm interested the Rockefeller Foundation in providing Wittgenstein with a research grant; he refused because he could not guarantee that he would be able to produce anything, and so the grant would have been accepted under false pretenses.[21]

Wittgenstein's deep concern with ethical matters is reminiscent of many religious figures. Here again, Malcolm sums up what becomes clear from the direct testimony of Wittgenstein and his friends. Though Wittgenstein was not religious, 'there was in him, in some sense, the *possibility* of religion.'[22] As usual this possibility carried over to the thoughts he wrote down; he remarked: 'I cannot help seeing every problem from a religious point of view.'[23] He understood religious impulses in a more than theoretical sense; and he 'took his hat off' to them.[24]

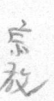

The 'possibility of religion' manifested itself in considerable reading of religious works, and this in a person who chose his reading matter very carefully. Drury's recollections include conversations about Thomas à Kempis, Samuel Johnson's *Prayers*, Karl Barth, and, many times, the New Testament, which Wittgenstein had clearly read often and thought about.[25] Wittgenstein had also thought about what it would mean to be a Christian. Some time during the 1930s, he remarked to Drury: 'There is a sense in which you and I are both Christians.'[26] In this context it is certainly worth noting that he had for a time said the Lord's Prayer each day.[27]

Wittgenstein's last words were: 'Tell them I've had a wonderful life!'[28] Even as close a friend as Norman Malcolm initially found this statement 'mysterious'; he felt that it did not square with the 'fiercely unhappy' character of Wittgenstein's emotionally and intellectually isolated existence.[29] Later, however, Malcolm recalled some impressions of Wittgenstein's many friendships and his joy in his work. When these factors are accentuated, his words do not seem so strange.

The picture of Wittgenstein we have built up so far can be enhanced by an examination of his direct relations with Kierkegaard. There are two kinds of material available which can give clues in this area. Most of the references are in memoirs by various friends and colleagues. Kierkegaard's name is also mentioned a few times in the selections from Wittgenstein's notebooks that have been published.

The first chronologically of the memoirs is this reminiscence by Paul Engelmann. It recalls conversations that took place in 1916 in Olmütz, Moravia, Engelmann's home town, where Wittgenstein was in artillery officers' training school.

> He 'saw life as a task'. . . . Moreover, he looked upon all the features of life as it is . . . as an essential part of the conditions of that task; just as a person presented with a mathematical problem must not try to ease his task by modifying the problem.[30]

This formulation reflects exactly Kierkegaard's position in the *Concluding Unscientific Postscript*: 'It is impossible that the task [of life] should fail to suffice, since the task is precisely that the task should be made to suffice.'[31] If life itself is set as a task, then it must be lived to the fullest.

What makes this reference particularly interesting is that Engelmann quotes Wittgenstein's exact words, which mirror Kierkegaard's both in letter and spirit; but there is absolutely no indication that Engelmann was aware of this parallel. It is hard to say whether Wittgenstein's expression of this existential understanding would be more striking if he had appropriated Kierkegaard so completely, or if he had developed such a view independently.[32]

The next reference to Kierkegaard is the following remark by Bertrand Russell, concerning his first meeting with Wittgenstein after the First World War:

RELEVANT BIOGRAPHY

I had felt in his book a flavour of mysticism, but was astonished when I found that he has become a complete mystic. He reads people like Kierkegaard and Angelus Silesius, and he seriously contemplates becoming a monk. It all started from William James's *Varieties of Religious Experience*.[33]

Wittgenstein never became a monk, of course, though he thought of doing so more than once, and did spend some time at monasteries. He might have been influenced by Kierkegaard's conviction that monastic retreat is a shirking of the 'task,' an abstraction from the conditions of existence.[34] But this report by Russell confirms that Wittgenstein was dramatically changed during the war, through his readings and perhaps through other events.

A rather later memoir comes from H. D. P. Lee, and dates from the period 1929–31 when Wittgenstein had returned to Cambridge. 'He told me that he learned Danish in order to be able to read Kierkegaard in the original, and clearly had a great admiration for him, though I never remember him speaking about him in detail.'[35] Certainly learning a new language suggests considerable interest!

An approving reference to the *Philosophical Fragments* finds its way into a conversation between Wittgenstein and Friedrich Waismann from December 1929: 'We thrust against the limits of language. Kierkegaard, too, recognized this thrust and even described it in much the same way (as a thrust against paradox).'[36]

There is a direct reference to *Either/Or* in the lecture notes (collated and published by students) from a course on religious belief which Wittgenstein gave in about 1938. In the context of a discussion of religious pictures of the world, and how they are manifest in life, he gave the following illustration:

> A great writer said that, when he was a boy, his father set him a task, and he suddenly felt that nothing, not even death, could take away the responsibility [in doing this task]; this was his duty to do, and that even death couldn't stop it being his duty. He said that this was, in a way, a proof of the immortality of the soul – because if this lives on [the responsibility won't die]. The idea is given by what we call the proof. Well, if this is the idea, [all right].[37]

RELEVANT BIOGRAPHY

This is a retelling of a story from the second part of *Either/Or*.[38] The depth of Wittgenstein's interest in Kierkegaard is reflected in his understanding of the anecdote as a piece of Kierkegaard's biography; scholars agree on this, but in the original it is presented as part of Judge William's letters.

Other details of Wittgenstein's knowledge of Kierkegaard are reported by Maurice O'C. Drury. During a discussion after a meeting of the Moral Sciences Club (so presumably during Wittgenstein's 1929–36 Cambridge period) Wittgenstein remarked: 'Kierkegaard was by far the most profound thinker of the last century. Kierkegaard was a saint.' He went on to mention the three stages of life. The stages are mentioned in two works he had certainly read, *Either/Or* and the *Postscript*. Drury also notes Wittgenstein's dissatisfaction with the literary style of the Lowrie translations of Kierkegaard. In later life, Drury recalls, Wittgenstein found the indirect method of Kierkegaard's works too prolix. 'When I read him I always wanted to say: "Oh, alright I agree, I agree, but please get on with it." '[39] This seems strange in view of Wittgenstein's own deliberately circuitous style!

A clue to his position here is provided by O. K. Bouwsma's recollections of a conversation with Wittgenstein in 1949. Bouwsma reports that Wittgenstein said he read Kierkegaard only in small pieces:

> He got hints. He did not want another man's thought all chewed. A word or two was sometimes enough. But Kierkegaard struck him almost as like a snob, too high, for him, not touching the details of common life. . . . (I'm not sure about his judgement here of Kierkegaard.)[40]

One possible explanation is that Wittgenstein was at a different 'stage' from Kierkegaard's intended audience.

The high esteem in which Wittgenstein held Kierkegaard is again shown in a letter from Wittgenstein to Norman Malcolm, dated 5 February 1948. Malcolm had mentioned *Works of Love*; Wittgenstein replies that he has never read that work. 'Kierkegaard is far too deep for me, anyhow. He bewilders me without working the good effects which he would in *deeper* souls.'[41] Wittgenstein's low moral self-esteem, as well as his admiration for Kierkegaard, is showing itself here.

In addition to these biographical notes, there are a few passages from posthumous collections that hint at a knowledge of Kierkegaard. In particular, several sections from the collection *Culture and Value* (which includes some of Wittgenstein's notes having to do with religion) mention him explicitly.

One reference, from the year 1937, again shows familiarity with the *Fragments* and *Postscript*. It is in the context of a discussion of the problem of the connection of historical proof and faith, and the possibility that the Gospels in all their want of historical precision and agreement are nevertheless the best possible form of communication of the Christian message. There is also mention of forms of expression appropriate to the various 'levels of devoutness.'[42] This again suggests familiarity with the *Stages* or *Either/Or*, at least. The particular combination of topics is also found in *Training in Christianity*.

Another context in which Kierkegaard is mentioned is that of the distinction between 'primordial' and 'tame' talent:

> In the same sense: the house I built for Gretl is the product of a decidedly sensitive ear and *good* manners, an expression of great *understanding* (of a culture, etc.). But *primordial* life, wild life striving to erupt into the open – that is lacking. And so you could say it isn't *healthy* (Kierkegaard). (Hothouse plant.)[43]

The exact reference here is unclear. Several of Kierkegaard's less-read works contain thoughts suggestive of parts of this remark. For example, the distinction between wild life and cultured manners suggests Kierkegaard's analysis, in his review of *Two Ages*, of the difference between the (passionate) 'age of revolution' and the (indolent) 'present age.'[44] Kierkegaard also praises Adler for having precisely what Wittgenstein feels his architecture lacks – some redeeming native spark.[45] Most specifically, in the *Christian Discourses* there is a prayer asking: 'if . . . we have lost our health, would that we might regain it by learning again from the lilies of the field and the birds of the air.'[46] But the thought has an unusual feel; there seems to be an admixture of original ideas, or ideas from another source: perhaps Nietzsche?

Finally, there is a reference to Kierkegaard in a group of entries from 1946. These notes have to do with having the courage to change one's life. Wittgenstein distinguishes here between cold wisdom or doctrine, and the ability to *embrace* it. He says: 'Wisdom is passionless. But faith by contrast is what Kierkegaard calls a

RELEVANT BIOGRAPHY

passion.'[47] This point of view is reminiscent of Wittgenstein's own sayings in the late pages of the *Tractatus.*

There are several interesting things about these direct references to Kierkegaard by Wittgenstein. First, they evidence a clear personal admiration for Kierkegaard as a thinker and a persuasive author. Second, it is important to note that they cover the whole length of Wittgenstein's career. The first references date from before the completion of the manuscript of the *Tractatus*; and his admiration seems if anything to deepen over the course of the 1930s. The last references, both from his notes and from others' recollections, are from the late 1940s. At the least this is evidence of a continuity in Wittgenstein's interest in the subject of religion and personal faith. The question of the relation between the *Tractatus* and the later philosophy must be considered in the light of this continuity. And there is also enough evidence to show that Kierkegaard's works can be a useful key to the understanding of Wittgenstein, at least in the matter of religion.

In addition to the instances of direct connections between Kierkegaard and Wittgenstein, there are two more very incidental mentions of a connection between the two thinkers. These have more to do with Wittgenstein's *demeanor* than with any traceable influence. Yet they are not wholly without interest when one remembers that Wittgenstein felt a close connection between his lifestyle and his philosophizing.

One of these references is very brief. Allan Janik records that Wittgenstein's tendency to approach everything 'from the ethical point of view . . . reminded [an Austrian acquaintance] directly of Kierkegaard.'[48]

Lastly, there is a more involved and fascinatingly indirect connection. K. E. Tranøy, a Norwegian student who came to know Wittgenstein in 1949, was impressed by Wittgenstein's knowledge of Ibsen's dramas, particularly *Brand*. Tranøy thought Brand's moral severity and human fallibility quite like Wittgenstein's.[49] But, as Lowrie confirms, Brand was a thinly veiled caricature of Kierkegaard and some of his unwelcome followers![50]

Of course neither of these two references carries much weight. They do serve to suggest the sense of absolute moral intentness common to both thinkers.[51]

RELEVANT BIOGRAPHY

KIERKEGAARD

At first glance, Kierkegaard's life seems to be remarkably different from Wittgenstein's. The differences begin with the form or texture of the two lives. While Wittgenstein's restlessness mirrored the aphoristic quality of his works, Kierkegaard led a remarkably settled existence. He was born in Copenhagen, and there he died. Aside from a few brief trips to Berlin, and a pilgrimage to his ancestral home in Jutland, he did not even venture from the province of Sjæland.[52]

But the geographically settled nature of Kierkegaard's life must be put in context. Wittgenstein was alternately drawn to the intellectual centers of Europe, and repulsed by them. He was better able to work in private and secluded places. Kierkegaard, for all his complaints that he was martyred as 'a genius in a provincial town,'[53] had in Copenhagen his scholarly retreat and town seat in one. As Lowrie points out, it was a small city of 200,000, but also a royal capital, with theater, library, and university.

Just as Wittgenstein's apparently fragmented existence renders biographical work a jigsaw puzzle, the stay-at-home character of Kierkegaard's life is reflected in the fact that his biographers have succeeded in giving a unified picture of him. But the reasons for this success are more complex than first appears. It is not that any public record of Kierkegaard's life was made; like Wittgenstein he had an intense sense of privacy. Rather, he was himself his own biographer. Nor does this autobiography exist in a wholly connected and honest form. But the pieces of the puzzle are, as it were, all collected in one box. There are also sketches in his published works that make parts of the pattern clear.

One work in particular gives an extraordinarily coherent interpretation of the main features of Kierkegaard's public literary production – his 'authorship.' *The Point of View for My Work as an Author*, written in 1848 (but published posthumously), explains his writings up to that point, and their connection to his life as publicly known, as a result of 'Divine Governance.' One of the questions which can only be answered through biographical inquiry is how he came to this understanding.

The intent of *The Point of View* is limited; and even within its limits the work is perhaps not completely honest.[54] But the gaps in

21

this published work are partly supplied by Kierkegaard's journals. Like Wittgenstein, Kierkegaard kept voluminous notebooks. But while the former confined his notes to philosophy (with a few exceptions), the latter made both biographical and reflective entries. It is a measure of Kierkegaard's astuteness at self-observation – and also of the close connection between his life and his literary production – that Walter Lowrie's biographies are nearly half direct quotes from the journals and published works.[55]

Because of this wealth of autobiography and reliable biography, the task of interpretation of Kierkegaard's life can be carried out somewhat differently than is the case with Wittgenstein. It is no longer mainly a question of assembling primary material coherently, but rather of singling out certain connections and facts relevant to the present task. One part of this project is finding clues to Kierkegaard's own understanding.

The journals are, among other things, a valuable document of the way in which published material came into existence. As is the case with Wittgenstein's notebooks, the seeds of published passages can often be seen in earlier journal entries; and indeed multiple drafts of works are sometimes represented.

But the real value of the journals lies in the fact that often biography and literary preparation are combined. Kierkegaard's talents as a psychological observer and 'spy' on himself and others allowed him to find universal themes in the particular happenings which he so astutely noticed.

The connection of the two most important personal relations in Kierkegaard's life with some essential categories used in his work is illustrated by the oft-repeated dedication and preface – which Kierkegaard published with each set of 'edifying discourses' he wrote, beginning in 1843. The discourses were dedicated 'to the memory of my deceased father Michael Pedersen Kierkegaard'; the preface emphasizes that the writer is 'without authority,' and indicates a desire that the works should find 'that individual whom with joy and gratitude I call *my* reader.'[56]

Kierkegaard's relationship with his melancholy father, and his own melancholy – partly a result of his father's melancholy – bore a large part in the instigation of his authorship. Kierkegaard summarized his father's case:

> How appalling for the man who, as a lad watching sheep on the
> Jutland heath, suffering painfully, hungry and exhausted, once

RELEVANT BIOGRAPHY

stood on a hill and cursed God – and the man was unable to forget it when he was eighty-two years old.[57]

This incident (and his subsequent rapid rise from poor lad to rich merchant, which convinced him that there really was a good God) gave Michael Kierkegaard such a sense of his own sin, and thus his son's original sin, that all of their relations were colored by it:

> From a child I was under the sway of a prodigious melancholy, the depth of which finds its only adequate measure in the equally prodigious dexterity I possessed of hiding it under an apparent gaiety and *joie de vivre*. So far back as I can barely remember, my one joy was that nobody could discover how unhappy I felt.[58]

Kierkegaard's talent for dissimulation may have been partly inherited from his father, who did not reveal the causes of his melancholy. Søren's sense of melancholy was heightened by his glimpsing of another part of his father's secret – his guilt over his relationship with his second wife. Kierkegaard reports it thus:

> Then it was that the great earthquake occurred, the frightful upheaval which suddenly drove me to a new infallible principle for interpreting all the phenomena. Then I surmised that my father's old-age was not a divine blessing, but rather a curse, that our family's exceptional intellectual capacities were only for mutually harrowing each other.[59]

But this realization led Kierkegaard closer to his eventual task:

> Inwardly shattered as I was, with no prospect of leading a happy life on this earth, . . . devoid of all hope for a pleasant, happy future – as this naturally proceeds from and is inherent in the historical continuity of home and family life – what wonder then that in despairing desperation I seized hold of the intellectual side of man exclusively, hung on to that, with the result that the thought of my eminent mental faculties was my only comfort, ideas my only joy, and men of no importance to me.[60]

Not only was Kierkegaard's literary production shaped by these circumstances of his youth; but his perception of his life's task was also molded by the sense that he was in some way bounded by the family guilt. (His pursuit of theology was a result of his father's wishes.) Furthermore he was not able to express this guilt and the religious purposes to which it led him – he was a captive of his 'inclosing reserve.'[61]

23

The second and more well-known example of the intertwining of Kierkegaard's life and work is the literary reflection of Kierkegaard's engagement to Regine Olsen. In this case his 'inclosing reserve' had tragic consequences.

Kierkegaard's involvement with Regine is related to his authorship in several and complex ways. First, the composition of *Either/Or* (the first work completed after the break), and particularly the 'Diary of the Seducer,' was explained by Kierkegaard himself as 'a good deed' in respect to her, to give an account of his motivations which would allow her to get over him.[62] The same might be said (in a more subtle sense) of *Fear and Trembling*, which contains passages fully accessible only to someone with an understanding which only Regine could have possessed at the time.

Both *Repetition* and 'Quidam's Diary,' a section of the work *Stages on Life's Way*, contain fairly direct references to Regine. The 'Diary' is perhaps the most personal, as it chronicles the deepest thoughts of the lover about his beloved – distanced by a year in time from the actual events. A brief section of *Repetition* reflects the relationship in an almost brutally dispassionate sense. This passage sets forth a project of using deception in order to break off a relationship, much more violent than Kierkegaard himself employed in relation to Regine. The project is proposed by a third party, and is so cold that the fictional lover cannot bring himself to put it into force.[63]

But the entire affair also had a more permanent effect on Kierkegaard's thought and work. This can be seen in the development of the phrase 'that individual.' He reported that the dedication to 'that particular individual, *my* reader,' which he first affixed to the *Edifying Discourses* which accompanied *Either/Or* in 1843, was composed with 'her' particularly in mind. But 'gradually this thought was taken over [assimilated],' and his concern for the individual rather than the crowd became an essential part of his authorship.[64] This is clear from the content of the two notes on 'the individual' which accompany *The Point of View*.[65]

At one point in his journals Kierkegaard even says that the development of the indirect method of communication was partly a result of his concern for Regine:

> Actually it was she – that is, my relationship to her – who taught me the indirect method. She could be helped only by an untruth

about me; otherwise I believe she would have lost her mind. That the collision was a religious one would have completely deranged her, and therefore I have had to be so infinitely careful.[66]

It was originally his 'inclosing reserve' which prevented the truth from coming out. But he later found a maieutic use for this reserve in the particular case of Regine; still later he generalized that use into his authorship.

Finally, Kierkegaard also believed that the intensity required for the completion of his literary/religious task was incompatible with the demands of the ethical state of marriage. His worries on this score are evident in a journal entry dated 2 February 1839 – a year and a half before the engagement. Even then, he wondered: 'Do the Orders say: March on?'[67]

So Kierkegaard's literary production may have been enhanced in several ways by the relation with Regine and its breakup: those circumstances provided him with material, with method, and also perhaps with the ability to concentrate (or lack of distractions) so necessary to the use of that material and method.

There is evidence of one other experience which decisively turned Kierkegaard to a religious expression of his talents. An entry in his journals runs thus:

> There is an *indescribable joy* that glows all through us just as inexplicably as the apostle's exclamation breaks forth for no apparent reason: 'Rejoice, and again I say, Rejoice.' – Not a joy over this or that, but the soul's full outcry 'with tongue and mouth and from the bottom of the heart': 'I rejoice for my joy, by, in, with, about, over, for, and with my joy' – a heavenly refrain which, as it were, suddenly interrupts our other singing, a joy which cools and refreshes like a breath of air, a breeze from the trade winds which blow across the plains of Mamre to the everlasting mansions.
>
> 10:30 a.m., May 19, 1838[68]

The generally agreed-on interpretation of this entry, dated with uncharacteristic precision, is that it reflects a mystical experience. Kierkegaard denied that he ever received authority from any such experience (in contradistinction to Magister Adler); but that is not to say that he did not have one. He merely wanted to make clear that he was not mystically aware of God's will, through revelation (as an apostle might be) – he saw himself instead under the category 'genius.'⁶⁹ Mysticism presents the double dangers of elitism and easy waiting for God to do everything.

At any rate the entry certainly reflects an experience of some kind; it recalls Wittgenstein's experience of 'wonder at the world.'⁷⁰

The talent for dissimulation, first learned by Kierkegaard as a mask for his melancholy (and which morbidly showed itself as his reserve), was another of the distinguishing marks of his life. He used it to good effect during the period of his 'aesthetic' production. The point was to have his apparent lifestyle in accord with the tone of the works which he was producing. As he reports in the *Point of View*, at times during the composition of *Either/Or* he was so busy that he had just a few minutes a day to spare; to get the best effect he would appear at the theater for five or ten minutes – and the gossips obligingly reported that he did nothing else every night!⁷¹

Dissimulation had another place in Kierkegaard's life. One of his few pleasures was his daily walk through Copenhagen. As Lowrie points out, the town was small enough for him to keep up with all developments of importance. By posing as a man-about-town, and exercising his considerable talents as a 'spy,' Kierkegaard gained the raw material which he transformed into the literary works.

Another category of Kierkegaard's authorship is his insistence that he was 'without authority.' This reflects his own religious status, which varied between his categories of 'infinite resignation' and 'Religiousness A.'⁷² He published a great many 'edifying discourses.' They were not 'sermons' because he did not have the authority of ordination. He wrote philosophical treatises (albeit well-disguised ones); but of course he lacked the authority of the systematic professor, and even that of the *privatdocent*. The Christian root of this category is clear: in his authorship as a whole he called individuals to a renewed sense of religiousness, but without pretending to lay claim to authority, which in a Christian sense could belong to only one Person (or at the very most three!).⁷³

Kierkegaard repeatedly stresses that the object of his work is very limited. He is not a systematic philosopher, but has a 'particular purpose.' The purpose is the investigation of 'what it means to become a Christian.'⁷⁴ It is essential to remember this because it may mean that some cases may be polemically overstated, and that some analyses may be incomplete (referring only to the religious use of a term).

The categories of 'the individual' and 'without authority,' which Kierkegaard derived from life, are closely related to this purpose. His uses of these categories are limited and polemical. Just as Kierkegaard did not claim any special status for himself (being without authority) so he particularly directed his writings to individuals regardless of their status. The next chapter will take up the larger implications of this form of address.

The relation between Kierkegaard's life and his authorship is the overriding example of his polemical task. Even in his private life he may have given events too much significance through reflection – it must not be forgotten that his diagnoses were self-diagnoses, since he was 'without authority' in the case of any other individual. But insofar as his public life was a polemical potentiation – a caricature, in which the features germane to the 'task' were emphasized – of his private life, it is the prime instance of his use of 'indirect communication.'

Finally, the relationship of 'Governance' to Kierkegaard's life must be discussed. In general, he understood his relation to this 'Governance' as like that of Socrates: 'he attended to himself – and then Providence proceeds to add world-historical significance to his ironical self-contentment.'[75] He felt in general that he had a 'task'; but the fulfillment of this task came through the building up of a pattern, the individual pieces of which did not make special sense at the time of their occurrence.[76]

But he had some sense of the unusual nature of his vocation quite early in his literary life. In *Repetition*, he used the category of the 'spy in a higher service.'[77] This is a complex idea. As articulated in the journals, it includes the notion of a reprehensible (sinning) past, and consequent obligation to God – as well as the more obvious ideas of dissimulation and the gathering of information.[78] 'The observer's job is to expose what is hidden,' as Constantin Constantius remarks. Only after many things are exposed can he see the pattern which guided these exposures.

PARALLELS

It remains to give some hints as to how the similarities between Kierkegaard's and Wittgenstein's lives affect our present task. The most obvious and general of these similarities is the understanding of the close connection of lifestyle and philosophical ideas.

The style of continual reworking and rethinking carries through to three areas of interest to us – the authors' personal lives, their literary production, and the style they advocated to others. But this reworking is shaped by a grounding ideal. The root of each man's unease lies in religious concern.

It might seem odd to make the claim that religion is an essential common feature of Kierkegaard's and Wittgenstein's lives. Certainly as an author Wittgenstein was not explicitly concerned with religion. Perhaps it would be more accurate to say that a religious search is a common element. Malcolm suggests that Wittgenstein had many times reached the point of crisis – at which Kierkegaard advocates the 'leap' – but *'could* not, or *would* not, "open his heart."'[79] At least he had a conception of a higher 'ethical' standard for the 'task' of life – a standard which he 'believed in,' but felt incompetent to fulfill.[80]

Kierkegaard carries the connection of life and works to a doubly-reflected extreme, since his works are rooted in his sin-consciousness, then a false moral expression is invented to aid in the proper interpretation of the works! Wittgenstein is not so explicit about the connection, but carries it out nonetheless. His philosophical 'brush-clearing' is partly an attempt to make plain the moral foundations of life; his attempts (and failures) to improve his own moral foundations have a great deal to do with the events of his life. He also attempted to impart these values to others – but not by explaining his own position; rather he tried to bring about the same soul-searching in his students that he himself had gone through. This method of working shows forth the anti-academic (or at least anti-doctrinal) streak which he shares with Kierkegaard.

Wittgenstein makes explicit a grasp of the close connection of ethical and aesthetic concerns which is also apparent in Kierkegaard's life. For both thinkers, what one makes of life depends in some measure on the 'aesthetic' principle or perspective from which one connects the various facets of the world. Both believe that this principle cannot be communicated directly.

Several similarities of method and understanding become clear within the basic framework of life-works connection. Kierkegaard, as the self-conscious biographer and psychologist, can provide some of the categories for the comparison. These categories will be important again and again in succeeding chapters.

Wittgenstein wanted to be 'without authority' in his teachings, just as Kierkegaard did. Although his closest friends understood him to be an extremely moral person, he did not so understand himself, and his protestations of personal inadequacy made him without moral authority. His rejection of academic forms was an attempt to escape scholarly authority. In the event, the 'first generation of disciples' allowed him both kinds of authority, despite his protestations. The moral component is now nearly lost, but unfortunately this is because the scholarly authority has been strengthened – in a direction opposite to that of morality.

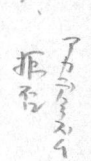

'The individual' is an accurate category for Wittgenstein as well. His works reflect this, as will be seen below. He always preferred to deal with one interlocutor in his philosophical talks. When Kierkegaard walked, he at least played the role of the *flâneur*; to walk with Wittgenstein was to be involved in serious philosophy, usually one-on-one. Even in his 'lectures,' he needed at least a friendly face to address.

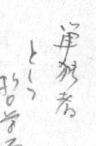

Finally, Wittgenstein believed in 'indirect communication.' This category is best discussed in connection with his writings; but it could be argued that his whole life was a communication of the way in which basic philosophy ought to be thought out and applied. At least he was conscious of the gap between the actual course of his life and his ideals; and he was apparently concerned that the actuality, rather than the ideals, would be 'communicated.' It must also be remembered that he successfully communicated philosophy in a house. '*Hausegewordene Logik*' is certainly an *indirect* communication!

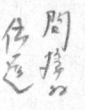

So far the 'Galtonian photograph' showing a type of philosopher is not complete. It is clear that both Kierkegaard and Wittgenstein believed that their lives and philosophies were intertwined more closely than usual. They also thought this intertwining right, and fostered it consciously. In fact, many of the tools which they brought to their authorships derived from the course of their respective lives. In each case, this is true of indirect communication, the address to the individual, and the refusal of authority.

But in order to flesh out the picture, as must be done before it can be fully evaluated, we should examine the works which were the fruits of these lives. If our authors are true to their principles, there will be a close connection between the methods and goals implicit in their lives, and those expressed in their works.

Chapter Two

METHODOLOGY

Both Kierkegaard and Wittgenstein are well known for having produced philosophical-literary works of an extraordinary kind. An interpretation of their intentions ought to take this into account.

Kierkegaard's 'authorship' (as he himself called it) includes a pseudonymous symposium in which various ideas and points of view are presented. It also includes the 'devotional addresses' and 'edifying discourses,' which are less often read; while they are not a remarkable form of writing in themselves (however remarkable they may be in content), when they are understood in connection with the pseudonymous works which they 'accompanied' – as part of the dialectic – they become part of a remarkable pattern. A third part of Kierkegaard's public writings is the 'attack' of his last months, which must also be seen in connection with the total *opus*. In addition to his writings, he saw his life as an important part of his communication (as has been suggested above).

The private material from his journals and papers conveniently shows the connection between his personal experience and the public works. As such it provides an added perspective on his work.

The form of Wittgenstein's writings is extraordinary for at least two reasons. The first is that there seem to be *two* 'authorships.' This idea is supported by Wittgenstein's own statements; in the later works he repeatedly refers to 'the author of the *Tractatus*' as though he were another person.[1] The second remarkable feature of Wittgenstein's production is that both parts of it are equally unusual experiments in communication. The *Tractatus* is notable for the logical rigor of its presentation. A unique point of view is single-mindedly presented – then matters are made more complex by the material on the 'ethical' and the 'mystical,' which (at first glance) does not fit with this single-minded presentation. The *Investigations* (and other collections published posthumously), on the other hand, show a discursive diversity of opinions and side issues. They also seem to be completely different in intention.

The private notes take on an added significance in Wittgenstein's case; since only the *Tractatus* was published by him (although the *Investigations*, and some other collections of notes, had clearly been edited with a view to publication) they are not merely an interesting source for an understanding of the private development of his thought. They are also the only guidelines for an attempt to grasp the general outline of his thinking in several related areas.

Neither author said much directly in the public forum about the objectives of his writing. But hints exist in various parts of the public works, and (particularly in the case of Kierkegaard) more than hints are available in the *Nachlaß*. This chapter will attempt to clarify the question of the authors' goals, by an investigation of the methods which they used. In both cases the two are bound up together.

One of the most important influences on the methods used by the two authors is their understanding of the place and limitations of 'philosophy.' Wittgenstein provides a succinct definition in the *Investigations*: 'Philosophy is a battle against the bewitchment of our intelligence by means of language.'[2] This thought can be related to two different bodies of material. The first connection is to the central battle which Kierkegaard fought, against the illusion that in 'Christendom' all are by definition 'Christians.'[3] Surely this is also a battle against bewitchment by means of language! Despite the similarity in appearance and derivation between the two words, they are only slightly related in the concepts they express: they have a 'family resemblance,' but they are distant cousins. A metaphor used by Wittgenstein is helpful here. The two concepts can be thought of as related in the same way as are the concepts 'railway train,' 'railway accident,' and 'railway law.' Although these all are complex concepts which have to do with railways, they are thoroughly different: one indicates an object, one a momentary event, and one a conceptual codification.[4] Similarly, 'Christendom' is a geopolitical relation, and 'Christianity' a spiritual state.

METHODOLOGY

The second direction in which the definition from the *Investigations* can be related is to the following passages from the *Tractatus*:

Philosophy aims at the logical clarification of thoughts.
 Philosophy is not a body of doctrine but an activity.
 A philosophical work consists essentially of elucidations.
 Philosophy does not result in 'philosophical propositions,' but rather in the clarification of propositions.
 Without philosophy thoughts are, as it were, cloudy and indistinct: its task is to make them clear and give them sharp boundaries. . . .
 It must set limits to what can be thought; and in doing so, to what cannot be thought.
 It must set limits to what cannot be thought by working outwards through what can be thought. . . .
 It will signify what cannot be said, by presenting clearly what can be said.[5]

Thus at the very beginning, Wittgenstein's definition changes the idea of 'philosophy.' A boundary wall is erected in the traditional subject matter of philosophy. Important things occur on both sides of the wall; but direct statements (sayings) can reach only one side. What is on the other side can only be 'signified' or 'shown.'

Kierkegaard saw a similar wall. The attempt to reach the other side of this wall is a constant temptation, as he notes:

[The] ultimate potentiation of every passion is always to will its own downfall, and so it is also the ultimate passion of the understanding to will the collision, although in one way or another the collision must become its downfall. This, then, is the ultimate paradox of thought: to want to discover something that thought itself cannot think. This passion of thought is fundamentally present everywhere in thought, also in the single individual's thought.[6]

For both Kierkegaard and Wittgenstein, philosophy is inevitable. But another essential feature of their thinking is that the place of philosophy is limited. It can do some preliminary brush-clearing and straightening out; but when it comes to the truly essential features, another kind of thinking is just as inevitably needed. They are both dedicated to demonstrating the presence of the wall, or 'ugly ditch' (Lessing); they are also dedicated to working toward getting beyond it.

An important kindred feature of both Kierkegaard's and Wittgenstein's thought at this point is their interest in limiting the scope of their discussions. That is, philosophy has a limited place within their total universes of discourse; but even these universes are limited in size. Kierkegaard puts this limitation most clearly; his entire work is

> related to Christianity, to the problem of 'becoming a Christian,' with a direct or indirect polemic against the monstrous illusion we call Christendom, or against the illusion that in such a land as ours all are Christians of a sort.[7]

In reading his works this must never be forgotten. Apparent gaps in his analyses may relate to the fact that they are only constructed for this particular purpose. (For instance, he explicitly says that his definition of truth as subjective only applies to 'the truth which relates to existence.'[8]) The authorship is a polemical corrective to the problems of the age. It may be recognized as such because it is opposed to the 'evil of the age.' Kierkegaard's championing of 'the individual' is a polemical result of the crowd mentality which he perceived in his age. Any good that there may be in that mentality (from a balanced view) is not his concern as a polemical, religious author.[9]

Kierkegaard's understanding of the place of philosophy in his task may be better understood when seen in comparison with his description of the power and way of working of the ironist, from *The Concept of Irony*: 'As the ironist does not have the new within his power, it might be asked how he destroys the old, and to this it must be answered: he destroys the given actuality by the given actuality itself.'[10] The biographical root of the method of indirect communication can be found in Kierkegaard's relation with Regine. But its philosophical antecedent is his work on Socrates. Like Socrates, he is able to demonstrate the inadequacies of philosophy by an ironic use of its own categories.

This also recalls Wittgenstein's way of working: 'the work of the philosopher consists in assembling reminders ["given" in the world] for a particular purpose.'[11] Wittgenstein's projects are also under a limitation similar to Kierkegaard's. The purpose of philosophy, according to him, is to eliminate itself! Wittgenstein's usual method is to get clear about particular 'philosophical' problems, and in so doing to show some features of philosophy in general. So his reminders may be various in their form. There may be polemical-corrective features in them; that is, if an idea is deeply entrenched, the reminders may have to be sharp beyond ordinary usage. And the reminders may also be *incomplete*. Wittgenstein's purpose in describing a situation or coining a term is not to give a systematically complete explanation or definition. Often he only notes the features germane to the point at hand. This arises from his task-orientation, and does not constitute a 'mistake' or oversight.

For both Wittgenstein and Kierkegaard, one particular problem demanding this unusual mode of thinking and communication is the ethical dimension of life. Wittgenstein's works also include explicit consideration of another essential feature requiring this other kind of thinking: the way in which language, thinking, and understanding work.

The key to this unusual kind of thinking and representation is contained in a brief statement by Wittgenstein: 'What *can* be shown, *cannot* be said.'[12] The logical and ethical dimensions are features which 'show themselves' in the world; but they are not directly expressible. Kierkegaard used the term 'paradox' to refer to human apprehension of such phenomena.

Paul Holmer suggests a way of looking at this inexpressibility which connects the early Wittgenstein both with his later works and with Kierkegaard. He points out that since certain dimensions 'cannot be said,' then the locus of certainty about them cannot be any doctrine. Instead, the thinker must be certain. 'Seeing is a capacity and can only be done by people, not sayings.'[13]

The theme of important material that is inaccessible to investigation is maintained through the later period. A key phrase used to refer to the problem is 'explanations come to an end somewhere.'[14] Nothing could be more essential than the features which do not require or permit explanation; it is precisely the fact that they are basic that makes them resistant to further analysis. As they are part of the framework of life, there are no tools available to get at them. Another key phrase is 'the limits of language.'[15] The later philosophy is concerned, as is the earlier, to show that there are certain games in which these limits ought to limit us, and certain games in which they may be (rightly) transcended – but also certain games in which they are in fact transcended, but wrongly or with infelicitous results. As Wittgenstein remarks, the existence of a wall or other boundary is not an unambiguous explanation of its purpose.[16] This may even depend on circumstances; jumping the tennis net is only a correct move after one wins the game. Wittgenstein takes metaphysical and other second-order attempts to explain the functioning of language to be unwarranted transcendences in an impossible direction; but he takes ethical statements to be permissible expansions.

Similarly, for Kierkegaard the attempt to philosophize *sub specie aeterni* is a wrong transcendence. It is wrong because it is forgetful of the existential situation and limitations of human beings. 'An existential system is impossible.'[17] On the other hand, the leap of faith is permissible, to say the least. Its permissibility is also rooted in the human existential situation – our need for assurance.

There is a feature of Kierkegaard's and Wittgenstein's methods which makes the task of studying them more difficult. This is that statements about the method and uses of the method are often intertwined. Paul Holmer observes concerning Kierkegaard that there are two kinds of sentences in his works. One kind expresses in linguistic form the immediate experience of a subject. Here, Kierkegaard's poetic bent shows itself. The other kind of sentence is one which deals with 'other sentences' or concepts. In this type of work Kierkegaard is at his most philosophical and analytic.[18]

This distinction is easy to see in the case of *The Point of View*, which consists largely of statements of the second kind. But the 'authorship' proper (both pseudonymous and acknowledged works) does not by any means consist only of statements of the first kind. Rather, in it they are liberally interlarded with philosophical and programmatic statements. It is often difficult to separate the two kinds. Indeed, sometimes the very same phrase seems to be both an existential or psychological observation, and a philosophical comment. This close connection of the two kinds of work reflects Kierkegaard's particular genius for rooting his writing in his own unified existence as a 'poet-philosopher.'

One of the best examples of this intertwining is the passage from the *Postscript* in which Johannes Climacus explains the principle of *his* 'authorship.' Climacus sets himself forth as an indolent student of philosophy. But one day while smoking a cigar in the public gardens, he has realized what he might be able to contribute to the well-being of the age. Since all the great people are making things easier and easier, it only remains for someone to make things more difficult, though of course not more difficult than they really are. This ironic project will be his life's work.[19]

This passage combines the indirect communication of an important principle of Kierkegaard's thought with the picture of Climacus, itself an indirect orientation as to how this work is to be taken. By the superposition over the course of a work of many such pictures and communications – a technique reminiscent of Wittgenstein's simile of the Galtonian photograph – Kierkegaard brings precision to his delineation of personality and philosophical position.

If this technique is a product of Kierkegaard's particular genius, certainly Wittgenstein shares his talent. Indeed, since in the case of Wittgenstein there is no parallel to *The Point of View*, the puzzle is even more complex. It is clear that Wittgenstein's works combine attacks on particular philosophical problems with his considerations of the possibility of philosophy; but the two tasks are not divided. More often than not, the same sentence does duty in the two endeavors. At least, the works themselves constitute a 'showing' of the correct way to do philosophy (while they 'say' things about various particular problems); and this is not at all a trivial showing since the form of the books is so radically different from that of previous philosophical works.[20]

An essential point about this method is that the same features evident in ordinary language use are used in philosophy. Holmer raises the question whether philosophical elucidations of grammatical distinctions might be neither sayings nor showings. He suggests that they constitute 'pointers' instead.[21] (At any rate, they would remain indirectly communicated.) The burden of this suggestion seems to be that philosophers call attention to language in a way not done every day. But pointing is a common phenomenon in which saying and showing are intertwined. It is even used as a method of proof: Wittgenstein was fascinated by the report that, for some Indian mathematicians, 'Look at this!' was a geometrical proof.[22] So there is no need to introduce philosophical 'pointing' as an absolutely special phenomenon.

Holmer is trying to make a fine distinction between philosophical and non-philosophical uses, one which Wittgenstein might not like, as it suggests a 'second-order' philosophical endeavor. Wittgenstein consistently denies that there is a 'second-level' 'philosophy of philosophy'; the discussion in this instance may be recursive (that is, one of the most common objects of philosophy is itself), but not second-order.[23]

One of the central methods used by the two authors is that of 'leading' the reader to a position. Wittgenstein remarks:

> We must begin with the mistake and transform it into what is true.
> That is, we must uncover the source of the error; otherwise hearing what is true won't help us. It cannot penetrate when something is taking its place.
> To convince someone of what is true, it is not enough to state it; we must find the *road* from error to truth.[24]

Kierkegaard agrees 'that if real success is to attend the effort to bring a man to a definite position, one must first of all take pains to find HIM where he is and begin there.'[25] Kierkegaard stresses psychological reasons for this manner of working: didactic prating is likely to make the listener ignore the message, and in the case of the message of 'becoming a Christian' this would be a tragedy. Wittgenstein's motivations are slightly different: keeping a solid anchor in reality is important to him principally for reasons of philosophical soundness, rather than due to any belief in the essential importance of his message.

The Point of View explains in great detail how this idea applies to Kierkegaard's works. He was always a religious writer; but he produced aesthetic works and philosophical works in an attempt to appeal to various kinds of readers. The fact that the 'Diary of the Seducer' has been published separately from the rest of *Either/Or* shows how successfully that part of the work mirrors aestheticism. The *Fragments* and the *Postscript* 'mirror' philosophy, not so much by their character as by the philosophical terminology and problems of which they make use. But at the same time, the various *Edifying Discourses*, written in an obviously religious form, exist as proof that he was always a religious writer.

The application of the idea of 'leading' to Wittgenstein's work is not so clear. One way in which it characteristically shows itself is within the individual works, or groups of notes. The remarks on the *Golden Bough* begin with Frazer's mistaken position, and attempt to show the outline of a better analysis of the facts he reports. The *Philosophical Investigations* begins with a passage from Augustine on language-learning. And *On Certainty* begins as a discussion of G. E. Moore's refutation of idealism: 'If you do know that *here is one hand*, we'll grant you all the rest.'[26]

What each of these works reflects is Wittgenstein's penchant for tackling one particular problem at a time, and worrying at it until he had gotten everything he could out of it. The individual works are not philosophies, or systems of philosophy: he once reacted violently when someone proposed that he should simply call the *Investigations* 'Philosophy.'[27] They are treatments of specific subjects.

At first glance, it might seem difficult to fit the *Tractatus* into this mold. It *appears* to be systematic and all-embracing. This appearance is particularly fostered by the fact that it is 'finished'; that is, it is not in the form of rough notes and discussions, as are the later works. The decimal numbering of propositions and the apparent purpose, to ground a scientific logic on a complete metaphysics, also support this impression. (And he himself calls it a 'system' in a letter to the publisher Ficker.[28])

Several considerations militate in the opposite direction. First of all, the *Tractatus* was written in reaction to the logical work of Russell and Frege. (It is interesting to note that neither of them understood it to Wittgenstein's satisfaction.) So it must at least start with logic if it is to follow his own methodology. Secondly, there is the evidence of Wittgenstein's own understanding of the scope and goal of the work. This is different from the first impression left by the text. The most straightforward expression of this understanding is given in another letter which he wrote to Ficker.

> It will probably be helpful for you if I write a few words about my book: For you won't – I really believe – get too much out of reading it. Because you won't understand it; the content will seem quite strange to you. In reality, it isn't strange to you, for the point of the book is ethical. I once wanted to give a few words in the foreword which now actually are not in it, which, however, I'll write to you now because they might be a key for you: I wanted to write that my work consists of two parts: of the one which is here, and of everything which I have *not* written.

And precisely this second part is the important one. For the Ethical is delimited from within, as it were, by my book; and I'm convinced that, *strictly* speaking, it can ONLY be delimited in this way. In brief, I think: All of that which *many* are *babbling* today, I have defined in my book by remaining silent about it.²⁹

Why would anyone write an ethical book that seems to be a logical book, so that those who are most likely to agree with it will not understand it? One possible explanation would be that those most likely to agree are not the intended audience. The audience suggested by the form of the book is logicians. If it is precisely some mistakes in logic that are preventing the logicians (and those influenced by them – in modern society, potentially a huge group!) from 'seeing things aright' ethically, and if the correct ethical view will have repercussions on their logical ideas, then in order to help them to find out the truth one must *lead* them from logic to ethics.³⁰

Without this understanding, the curious form of the *Tractatus* seems even more curious when it is compared to the form of the notebooks which Wittgenstein kept at the time he was composing it. These notebooks are in the style which is familiar in the works of the later Wittgenstein, rather than in any systematic style. They reflect his discursive struggle to understand the issues. The material on the 'ethical' in the final form of the book is presented in a form most similar to that of the notebooks. This suggests that the style of the *Tractatus* is purposely artificial. Not only is it an expression of the best of the material from the notebooks (or of the position finally reached); this expression has been cast in a style which relates to a particular purpose.³¹

In the preface to the *Philosophical Investigations*, Wittgenstein explains that he has been unable to develop that work into a unified form, as he had at first wanted.³² But he realized that the somewhat discombobulated style is appropriate to a technique which consists in multiple methods for various problems.³³ The form of the *Tractatus* is appropriate to a technique which promotes one understanding as the solution to all problems.³⁴

All of these features point toward an expansion of the idea of 'finding the reader where he is.' Once one has done this, then some technique must be devised for getting the reader to progress. A didactic method will not be useful, since it assumes the correctness of the speaker's position.

Kierkegaard called the method which he used in a similar situation 'indirect communication.' As he claims in *The Point of View*, the whole of his work is related to the 'problem of becoming a Christian.' But at first glance, the larger part of his literary production has little to do with this problem. Instead, he describes the life of the aesthete and the ethicist from within, and apes the writings of the philosopher. The purpose of this description is nevertheless consistent with his project.

In a series of notes for lectures on communication, Kierkegaard distinguishes between the appropriate methods for communicating 'science' and 'art.' Science or specific knowledge of content must be communicated directly; art, ability, or potential competence, on the other hand, is already within the subject, and hence must be taught in another way. It is a question of 'luring the ethical out of the individual,' rather than 'beating it into him.' The indirect communicator stands in a 'maieutic' relationship to the listener. He is not imparting any new knowledge; instead he is bringing something out in the other. As Kierkegaard says, 'the object of the communication is . . . not a knowledge but a realization.'[35]

The 'midwife's' role in this case is very delicate. It is a question of maintaining the distinction between 'standing by another's help alone' and 'standing alone – by another's help.' Clearly the second, ironic alternative is the one aimed at. The midwife is attempting to give an advantage – but if the one helped has any idea that he is being helped, then that may become a disadvantage.[36] So it is that the indirect communicator must somehow manage to touch the intended recipient of the communication without revealing himself. As Kierkegaard says elsewhere, he must pass him going in the opposite direction and yet somehow manage to give him a push!

The expressed purpose of the *Tractatus* is to show that 'what can be said at all can be said clearly, and what we cannot talk about we must pass over in silence.' In order to achieve this purpose, problems of philosophy are discussed (said), and it is shown 'that the reason why these problems [of philosophy] are posed is that the logic of our language is misunderstood.' But part of the value of the work is yet another showing: 'it shows how little is achieved when these problems are solved.'[37] There is a direct and an indirect part to the results.

Two very important explicit parts of the scheme of the *Tractatus* (as well as the whole scheme of showing) have to do with the need

METHODOLOGY

for indirect communication. The first concerns the status of logic. Logical form, as the form of propositions and the world, does not exist in the world and cannot be expressed in words. 'Logic is not a body of doctrine, but a mirror image of the world.'[38] It makes the whole scheme of language possible. While occurrences within the world are 'accidental,' and could be otherwise, the logical framework is fixed. It is nonsensical to make statements about something which cannot be otherwise: there is no point of comparison. Thus logic cannot be discussed.

Ethical considerations are also bound up with indirect communication. Here the indirection is double: not only are ethical propositions not candidates for direct expression (according to the *Tractatus*); but the very communication of this fact is itself indirect. The ethical content of the world cannot be expressed in words; like logic it is 'not part of the world.' Just as logic cannot be 'accidental,' so values (if they are to escape relativism) must not depend on 'what is the case.'[39] This analysis squares with Kierkegaard's thesis 'attributable to Lessing' that accidental truths of history cannot serve as proofs for eternal truths of reason.[40]

Both the phenomena of logic and values are said to be 'transcendental.'[41] This is certainly not to say that they do not exist; but they cannot be directly discussed. By discussing the way in which the world is constructed and mirrored in language, Wittgenstein is indirectly showing the importance of those things which cannot be spoken about. The strictly correct way of doing philosophy, he says, would be to say only what *can* be said. This method would be even more indirect than the method which he actually uses.

Wittgenstein's actual method is to make statements which are (strictly speaking from within the final result) nonsensical.[42] The listener's role is to 'transcend' these propositions, in order to reach a vantage point from which he can 'see the world aright.'[43] This remains an indirect mode of communication.

Thus there is a redoubled indirection in the communication of the *Tractatus*. First of all, the ethical purpose is hidden behind the logical appearance of the work. Secondly, the logical apparatus is incapable of carrying its own weight. It does appear to be a direct communication; but on the metaphysical level it cannot be one. The foundations of logic, too, ought to be indirectly communicated.

A modification of the doctrine of indirect communication is at

41

work in Wittgenstein's later works. He repeatedly denies that philosophical points can be made by the advancing of 'theses.'[44] Theses can only be about facts, and so everyone would agree to them; it would be impossible to have arguments and various positions. Philosophy is not concerned to give new information, as do the sciences, for example. Instead, it is concerned with 'putting everything before us,' 'assembling reminders,' with the aim of complete clarity. The ideal way of gaining clarity, for the later Wittgenstein, is the method of 'perspicuity': 'arranging the factual material so that we can easily pass from one part to another and have a clear view of it.'

> For us the conception of a perspicuous presentation is fundamental. It indicates the form in which we write of things, the way in which we see things. . . .
>
> This perspicuous presentation makes possible that understanding which consists just in the fact that we 'see the connections.' Hence the importance of finding *intermediate links*.[45]

If 'a philosophical problem has the form "I don't know my way about," '[46] then perspicuous presentation is intended to suggest an arrangement or map of the facts, to remove the confusions. Or, if philosophy is to be treated like a sickness,[47] then the various methods of the philosopher, which clarify the problems, are like various therapies.[48]

That this is a doctrine of indirect communication should be clear. Direct communication proceeds by the advancing of theses. These are appropriate to science. But philosophy cannot communicate directly. Instead, by arranging what we already know[49] the philosopher makes problems disappear. Of course, the satisfaction of the answer is not communicated; every reader or listener must examine and agree with the proposed 'solution.'

Kierkegaard shares with Wittgenstein the interest in a way of working which stresses the transitions rather than the theses. His interest in the polemical and corrective is a good indication of this. But it is easy to forget the stress on transitions when confronted with a 'system' like that of the 'stages on life's way.' Kierkegaard takes care to delineate the operators of the transitions between the stages. The transition between the aesthetic and the ethical is marked by irony, and the transition from the ethical to the religious by humor.

METHODOLOGY

Both humor and irony depend on the clash of perspectives. To see a situation as humorous depends on the ability to step out of it, to see it as another might. The inclosing seriousness of a perspective is shattered. Then there is the possibility that a new perspective can be gained.

Kierkegaard places considerable stress on these transitional categories, although in view of the fact that his dissertation was about the concept of irony in both ancient and modern times, this is not surprising. Wittgenstein has much less to say about them in a theoretical vein. He does comment that the 'depth' of grammatical jokes is like that of philosophy.[50] And Malcolm notes that Wittgenstein had once claimed that it would be possible to write a serious philosophical work consisting solely of jokes.[51] But the principal evidence of his understanding of the importance of these phenomena in changing one's way of looking at the world lies in the (often heavy-handed) irony and sarcasm of many of his remarks. For instance, in dissecting the grammar of sensations, he answers the assertion 'Well, I *believe* that this is the sensation S again' by remarking 'Perhaps you *believe* that you believe it!'[52]

The importance of disturbing presuppositions is also expressed in Wittgenstein's desire to transform 'disguised nonsense' into 'patent nonsense.'[53] Once nonsense is recognized as such, it will be much easier to reject. Humor and irony are excellent methods of beginning this recognition.

The feature of language which Wittgenstein thinks susceptible to these clarifying techniques is what he calls its 'grammar.' The kind of reminders he uses are reminders of the way in which the language is used every day; 'philosophical problems arise when language goes on holiday.'[54] One basic type of misunderstanding is that which arises when the surface appearance of a linguistic structure is different from its actual usage – a conflict between the 'surface grammar' and the 'deep grammar.'[55] For instance one might be tempted to group 'games' together just because they all are given that name; Wittgenstein reminds us of the variety of phenomena that lurk beneath the common name.[56]

Wittgenstein's dependence on 'everyday language' is subtle. He is interested in what he or others may be 'inclined to say.' But such an inclination or temptation is merely raw material; the surface inclination may mask a deeper confusion, and this is the province of philosophical 'treatment.'[57]

Kierkegaard's psychological investigations perform a similar function. He is recalling people from flights of systematic or religious fancy by recalling the forgotten circumstances of everyday life. Although Christianity might seem to be just another possible life-style, Kierkegaard reminds his audience that it is 'deeply' different. It is different because it claims to address the central existential question of finitude.

The mention of 'intermediate links' in the quotation on p.42 deserves further examination. Such links are an important feature of both Kierkegaard's and Wittgenstein's work. In both cases the links proposed often take the form of stories or invented situations. Two cases are shown to be similar in that they share features with a third case. Here one might recall Wittgenstein's concept of 'family resemblance.' But it is not as though these links have any real life of their own. It is the formal connection between existing cases that is interesting; the link calls attention to the similarity, and at the same time (like 'family resemblance') emphasizes the differences. The links and parables are attempts to call attention to the way of seeing being put forward.[58]

Important reflections of this technique occur in two of the central discussions of the *Investigations*: that of 'now I understand, now I can go on' and that of the phenomena of 'seeing' and 'seeing-as.' These discussions also reflect the typical intertwining of philosophical reflections on methodology and the use of this methodology on other problems.

The material concerning 'now I understand' begins at section 143 of the *Investigations*. One part of the point of this discussion is an elucidation of the grammar of 'to know' and allied concepts. The surface grammar makes us think that 'knowing' or 'being able' is a particular thing or experience that accompanies the performance of correctly continuing a required series. In fact (on closer observation) it is not even the case that some particular content is connected with this performance. An interesting example is the sudden grasping of a crossword answer. The feeling of ability to write the correct word often comes before the word itself; the pen starts moving toward the paper before the word comes to mind explicitly.[59] Being able to continue is often the result of 'having a technique,' which of course does not indicate any continuous state of conscious mind.

METHODOLOGY

The point of this discussion as it affects the present argument is that there is not necessarily any additional content which suddenly makes understanding or continuing a series possible. In making the correct arrangement of a jigsaw puzzle, the 'scheme' of the puzzle does not necessarily enter in; rather, the arrangement simply is made. Reasons for choosing a particular answer to a crossword need not be explicit or new information. The usual way in which we solve problems is a good model of the use of the idea of 'perspicuous presentation,' which works for Wittgenstein both in everyday life and in philosophy.

Kierkegaard's idea of the 'perspective of faith' fits well with this model of problem-solving. When a thinker has encountered the Absolute Paradox, there is no further factual information to be gained. It is precisely for this reason that he experiences the Paradox. This paradox cannot be abrogated or sublated (*aufgehoben*); it can, however, be transformed (by the perspective of faith) from a negative to a positive phenomenon.

The discussion of the grammar of the word 'see' occupies most of section xi, the longest section of part two of the *Investigations*. Intertwined in normal usage are the photographic 'seeing' which would permit a copy to be made, and the gestalten 'seeing' (or fossilized 'seeing-as') which determines the place assigned to a thing in our thought-world. While the first image may remain the same, the second report may change. Such an optical illusion as a two-dimensional representation of a cube, for example, may be seen as first a cube, and then a concave shape. On the other hand, sometimes only one aspect is noticed.

The phenomenon of aspects may recur on many different levels. The most basic is that of applications of a picture. As Wittgenstein points out, the same two-dimensional cube figure might represent several things: a glass cube, a wire frame, three boards nailed together.[60] Other clues in the context are important in determining the interpretation.

Another level of aspects of situations and presentations is their state of fluidity or solidity. Optical illusions are purposely constructed with a lack of contextual cues, so that the interpretation remains fluid. But we tend to see only one aspect of everyday objects. One which may serve as an example is a mirror. We do not 'take it as' a mirror (as we may 'take' the two-dimensional representation of a three-dimensional object in more than one way); rather, it just *is* a mirror. Yet once we had to learn that it was a mirror, and what could be done with it (what Wittgenstein would call its 'grammar'). A child or a primitive may fail to understand the 'physical grammar' of this object. For ordinary adult persons, at some point the possibility of seeing it differently has been eliminated. In the future, this possibility may need to be reinstated, somewhat as, in a familiar animal-behavior experiment, the monkey can reach the bananas if it can understand a set of boxes as stairs.

Philosophical problems have many features in common with the case of the mirror. They are traditionally seen in a certain way. But the way in which they are seen may not be appropriate; it may be problematic. Then the problem of the philosopher is first to re-fluidize the understanding of the problem, and then to change the way in which it is understood. This must be done indirectly. A fork might well be used as a garden tool, but one cannot simply claim that an heirloom silver fork is a garden tool; one must be convincing. This is partially because there is no separate 'knowing' which can be adduced to prove the possibility of this use; there is no additional information to be given. But certain aspects of the situation must be emphasized – perhaps the urgent need for shipwreck survivors to plant seeds for food on a desert island.

Kierkegaard's objective with regard to the concept 'Christian' is of a similar kind. The understanding of the word has become canalized in a bad direction. Through his polemic, he hopes to recall the Gospel grammar of the concept.[61]

Both Wittgenstein and Kierkegaard were interested in the rejection of pat answers. The 'task' of Johannes Climacus, quoted above, will serve as a convenient representation of Kierkegaard's thoughts on this matter. Those who were 'making things easier' in philosophy and religion in his time were the Hegelian systematists. And Wittgenstein had the same concern about the professional philosophers. They promised complete understanding, a 'crystalline system.' But the twofold problem with this idea is that the idea is flawed and (partly as a result) 'philosophy' cannot deliver as advertised. The *Investigations* are messier in appearance than the *Tractatus*; things are made more difficult; but not more difficult than they really are. The solution, while of a different kind than that proposed by a system, is no less final once grasped.

The ideal of the task of convincing brings up another important point of contact between the methodologies of Kierkegaard and Wittgenstein. They both focused their efforts on the individual. This focus can be clearly seen in the prefaces to Wittgenstein's works. That of the *Investigations* says: 'I should not like my writing to spare other people the trouble of thinking. But, if possible, to stimulate someone to thoughts of his own.'[62] And the first paragraph of the preface to the *Tractatus* reads:

> Perhaps this book will be understood only by someone who has himself already had the thoughts that are expressed in it – or at least similar thoughts – so it is not a textbook. Its purpose would be achieved if it gave pleasure to one person who read and understood it.[63]

These formulations clearly recall the emphasis which Kierkegaard places on the individual reader. There are good reasons why they should. First, both authors are communicating indirectly. As was suggested above, the nature of that enterprise is such that every individual reader must be independently convinced of the proposed improvements in understanding. A directly communicated work – a scientific text – can be relied upon. The material in it is factual, and has been derived according to various laws and standards. As Wittgenstein says, the content of 'theses' must be acceded to by all. But a perspicuous presentation of the facts, designed to alter someone's view of the world, can only be accepted or rejected by each individual.

Kierkegaard's understanding of this method is demonstrated when he talks of 'appropriation' and 'double reflection.' These two categories stress the role of the person on the receiving end. Indirect communication is doubly reflected. The communicator reflects on the problem, and makes an attempt at communication. The listener must also reflect, and his reflection governs the way in which he will appropriate the material. The dialectic of double reflection is explained in his material on 'the listener's role in a devotional address' in *Purity of Heart*.[64] It is also shown – in fact, perhaps best shown – by the development of his own case. He remarks in a journal entry:

> It must above all be pointed out that I am not a teacher who originally envisioned everything and now, self-confident on all

points, uses indirect communication, but that I myself have developed during the writing. This explains why my indirect communication is on a lower level than the direct, for the indirectness was due also to my not being clear myself at the beginning. Therefore I myself am the one who has been formed and developed by and through the indirect communication.[65]

This passage provides a link between 'indirect communication' and the category of 'the individual,' which is also closely related to 'the problem,' Kierkegaard's task. It must not be forgotten that his use of this category is limited and polemical.

Gregor Malantschuk provides an interesting analysis of four terms which Kierkegaard uses for individual humans. The lowest term is *Exemplar*, indicating a specimen, copy, or member of a crowd. Next stands the individual (*Individ*), who is not simply a member of the species or herd in an animal sense, but nevertheless remains dependent on his heredity and environment. Third is *Individualitet*, conscious self-choice. The highest category is 'the single individual' (*den Enkelte*), who is the 'self grounded transparently in God' of *The Sickness Unto Death*.[66] The flavor of this term accords well with Wittgenstein's term of approbation, 'human being.'

Although Kierkegaard's dedications are to *Hiin Enkelte* (originally meant to refer to Regine), in the context of his own understanding of his task this term has a double meaning. Many of the pseudonymous works effect their results through pictures of extraordinary individuals, or archetypes. In the *Edifying Discourses*, rather than the person of position it indicates the potential within everyman. The thrumming of this dialectical tension will at least serve, like a noisemaker, to call attention to the importance of the category.[67] But even when Kierkegaard is talking about 'everyman,' this is not to say the 'crowd'; the mentality of the crowd, which easily does things that no individual would do, is 'untruth.'[68] The authorship is directed to each and not to all: to *Hiin Enkelte* and not to the *Exemplar*.

The importance of the term for Kierkegaard's 'task' is related to the illusion he sought to destroy, that 'all are Christians of a sort.' The category 'individual' is the 'narrow defile' through which any Christian must pass. It is essential for those who would become Christian, and so getting the category noticed must be one of Kierkegaard's highest priorities.[69]

The 'Socratic' nature of the enterprise being carried out by each author reflects another facet of the dedication to the individual. Quite aside from the idea of 'Socratic method,' or asking leading questions (which is practiced by both), there is a similarity between the way in which they generated their thoughts and the way in which Socrates worked. Kierkegaard comments in his dissertation that the Academy essentially consisted in a group of people sitting around watching Socrates think.[70] It is hard to imagine a more apt description of Wittgenstein's classes. His published works all follow the same pattern. Even the *Tractatus*, which was polished so far beyond the notebook form, is merely a compilation of 'that which really occurred to me – and how it occurred to me.'[71] The *Investigations* and some of the other works were polished to some extent, but they retain the form of internal dialogue and attempts at convincing oneself.

Kierkegaard's works, of course, also follow the same pattern. Through the intervention of 'Divine Governance' the working out of his personal thoughts and difficulties was projected into the task of explicating 'becoming a Christian.'

Kierkegaard's understanding of the idea of governance is an ironical one. It involves his looking back over his life and noting the plan. Like Socrates, he found 'world-historical significance' superimposed on his struggles by Providence. His doings had one significance to him, but turned out to have an expanded significance to the world. The same might be said of Wittgenstein.

All this is of course not to deny that the works of Kierkegaard and Wittgenstein have a larger relevance. In fact, this relevance is stressed by both. Much of it is derived from the personal relevance which the works had first. The authors felt that the works could only acquire any possible larger relevance piecemeal, by becoming relevant for individuals.

This is one of the roots of a final Kierkegaardian category, 'without authority.' Kierkegaard defines authority as 'a specific quality which, coming from elsewhere, becomes qualitatively apparent when the content of the message or of the action is posited as indifferent.'[72] As has been mentioned in chapter 1, Kierkegaard did not claim any authority for his work. His was a peculiarly dialectical position. He was without temporal authority (because not ordained) and without eternal authority (because not a prophet or an apostle). Nevertheless he found his 'genius' – his natural talent – to be 'daimonically' guided by 'Divine Governance.' His whole life was willy-nilly an indirect communication.

METHODOLOGY

In the foregoing material some features of a method have been presented. They center around various common themes: the place of philosophy, the polemical task, the address to the individual, the stress on transitions, the necessary use of indirect forms of communication, the recognition of the phenomenon of perspective, the refusal of didactic authority. Some of these categories are more clearly articulated by Wittgenstein; some are better expressed by Kierkegaard. Both thinkers can be understood in these terms. Each did actually understand his own work in these terms to some extent.

But the limits of the method which these features delineate cannot be exactly specified. One more category may be useful in explaining this vagueness.

A feature of phenomena that impressed Wittgenstein was their almost infinite *suggestiveness*. He discussed this category explicitly in connection with two great interpreters of the human experience, Frazer and Freud. He was critical of both thinkers, and for a similar reason: they were reluctant to allow the possibility of diverse interpretations of phenomena. Freud's insistence on *the* one correct interpretation of dreams and jokes was discussed in various lectures and conversations.[73] Frazer's tendency to see magic as 'wrong science' and to claim that our interpretations of traditions depend on their historical development received similarly short shrift.[74]

This reluctance to agree to the existence of single correct and causally based interpretations is reflected in the nature of Wittgenstein's own work – and in Kierkegaard's. What is being put forward is not one particular point of view, but many suggestions that tend toward a kind of viewpoint. (Not one face, but a Galtonian composite.) Only the reader can connect the given examples into a way of thinking and life. Wittgenstein remarks that he is attempting to change the 'style of thinking' (or to persuade others to change their style of thinking).[75]

The style of the two authors' works clearly reflects their 'style of thinking.' The same problem is often approached from a variety of viewpoints. Quite ordinary phenomena become extraordinary when seen in the appropriate contexts. But the immediate context of a remark is not always its only fruitful context. This is certainly true of the 'Diary of the Seducer,' for example. And it is also true of Wittgenstein's remarks. His struggles over their arrangement often resulted in the inclusion of the same remark in more than one manuscript. Nor is it merely a question of weakness or indecisiveness; the remarks actually contribute to a variety of discussions. The decimal numbering of the *Tractatus* is an invitation to read the remarks in a variety of sequences, or to a variety of depths. At one time Wittgenstein actually thought of connecting the remarks in the *Investigations* with a 'network' of numbers.[76] In short, both authors' works are 'hypertexts' which guide the reader, but require an active construction at the time of reading.[77]

But this shared understanding of the way in which ideas could be communicated has led to problems in the understanding of the upshot of their works. Kierkegaard has been called an irrationalist and a fideist, and said to promote a purely subjective ideal incompatible with social institutions like the established church. Wittgenstein has been called a fideist and a relativist, and has been seen to promote a purely *social* ideal in reaction to the traditional concept of the subject. The next chapter will attempt to sort out some of these assertions, and to give some idea of the kind of position that one might come to by aid of their methods.

Chapter Three

PROBLEMS OF INTERPRETATION

The special nature of the methods used by both Kierkegaard and Wittgenstein makes the task of interpreting and applying their works particularly difficult. In fact, the first problem is whether 'interpretation' and 'application' are the appropriate categories in which to examine their concerns. Insofar as they both spoke to particular individuals concerning the particular therapies appropriate to particular problems, it would seem ironic at best to attempt to abstract some general principles which could be followed in various cases. It is especially hard to imagine what an interpretation of such a particularized therapy would be. Both authors stress the limits of possible explanation, as will be seen below.

Two forms of 'interpretation,' which often create problems in the attempt to understand other writers, are especially dangerous in the cases of Kierkegaard and Wittgenstein.

The first of these problematic methods is the tendency to think of the works as containing, or at least sketching, a 'systematic philosophy.' Such a system would have room for particular theoretical positions on most of the traditional questions of philosophy: a general ethics, an epistemology, a metaphysics, and so forth.

The second dangerous principle of interpretation has in common with the first that it tends toward 'system.' But rather than interpreting the existing work as systematic, this method operates in a more insidious way. It consists in taking some fragments of the author's work out of context, reifying a systematic theory from them, and using that to generate 'the author's position' on a given topic.

Both of these principles of interpretation can be seen at work in the most common understandings of two points essential to Kierkegaard's and Wittgenstein's authorships. One of these points is the relative importance of the individual subject and society. A closely related field is their understanding of the relations between different societies or worldviews. An investigation of the way in which the authors themselves approached these issues may shed light, not only on the issues, but also on the possibility of 'interpretation' and 'extension' of their work.

The tendency to reify theories is especially evident in interpretations of one of the most famous portions of the *Philosophical Investigations*, the so-called 'Private Language Argument.' It is particularly significant of the danger here that there is some disagreement about the exact portion of the text which should be counted as belonging to the 'argument'! There are no definite boundaries in the text. (This is a by-product of the 'Galtonian photograph' writing style, in which the *whole text* is needed in order fully to support any one portion of it.) But the first indexed use of the term 'private' occurs at section 243, and the discussion of rule following and 'knowing how to go on' picks up after about section 320.

The mere fact that this discussion is called the 'Private Language Argument' may well produce some expectations about its content. Surely it must have to do 1) with language; 2) with a *private* language, that is, one available only to a single individual. Furthermore, a cursory knowledge of Wittgenstein's general disposition suffices for one to be fairly sure that he would be 'against' the idea of private languages. He often speaks of 'language-games,' and the paradigm of games is social.[1] His term 'form of life,' which appears (among other places) just before the beginning of the section on privacy, also expresses a clearly social idea.

The expectation which this background information raises is that the argument is a reaction to a thing which has been proposed. This thing is a language, like languages we have all experienced and used. It is also private – it is the protocol of an internal dialogue. However, Wittgenstein is against it on evidential grounds. He relegates it to the status of 'the present king of France,' or better 'the third eye in the middle of my forehead.' This physiognomic innovation would have its uses, but – unfortunately – it does not exist.

PROBLEMS OF INTERPRETATION

Such an interpretation of Wittgenstein's position necessarily reduces the value of the individual subject in her subjectivity. If there is no language for internal reports, then (to take a positivistic line of argument) there can be no 'subject.' Only what is speakable is real, and only what is public is speakable; so only what is public is real – only the social dimension counts.

This understanding of Wittgenstein's intentions does not take into account the nature of his interest in phenomena. He remarks that philosophical investigations are conceptual in nature, and the classic error of metaphysics is that it confuses factual and conceptual work.[2] Then if indeed Wittgenstein is 'against' 'private language,' it will not be that he finds such a thing to be conceivable (but contingently nonexistent); rather it will be because the whole conceptual scheme suggested by the idea 'private language' is wrong. Then the question 'can there be a private language?' will not be settled, but eliminated. This will be true because the model of 'language' will be shown to be inapplicable at this point.[3]

The difference between Wittgenstein's method and factual investigation is suggested by a metaphor he himself used. Rather than resolving an argument as one would release the tension from a spring, he proposes to dissolve the argument as one would dissolve the spring in acid![4] The metaphor neatly illustrates his intention to work in a different dimension.

A clue that the 'Private Language Argument' might reject a whole conceptual scheme is already available in section 244 of the *Investigations*, at the very beginning of the 'argument.' There Wittgenstein remarks that 'the verbal expression of pain replaces crying and does not describe it.' Both crying and saying 'Ouch!' are 'pain-behaviors'; but the verbal expression is learned.

The problem addressed arises because of a conflict between the surface and deep grammars of certain expressions of pain. Exclamations are fairly primitive linguistic pain-behaviors. Far more sophisticated ones exist. Even on the next possible level an instantaneous utterance such as 'That hurts!,' the apparent form is that of a report. And a much used example, 'I have a toothache,' even makes it sound as if there were a thing (genus *pain*, species *toothache*) that is the object reported. From these cases it is easy to suppose that 'Ouch!' and crying are also 'reports' about what 'I know.'

A closer examination of the complex expressions ('in the

language game which is their home') reveals that they do not function like the simple declarative sentences they emulate. This is easy to see if we assume they are sentences in the 'game of information' and try to use them as such.

Jane: I've got five dollars.
Harry: I'm from Missouri; you'll have to show me!
Jane: (taking out her wallet) Here they are.

Paul: I've got a headache!
Tom: Wow! Can I see, huh? Huh??
Paul: ??!!?!?

Jane can easily produce physical evidence to back up her assertion. But Paul could at best produce symptoms. This kind of gap is totally unacceptable in sensation statements. Rather than being the kind of propositions which can be objectively only true or false (though perhaps psychologically or statistically probable, uncertain, highly doubtful), statements like Paul's are *indubitable* – '*that* is how we use it. (And here "know" means that the expression of uncertainty is senseless.)'[5]

As the 'argument' continues, Wittgenstein's intentions are clouded by his methodology. There is a long discussion of whether it would be possible for someone to name privately a sensation, 'S,' and keep track of the occurrences of this sensation. This begins to look like a factual investigation. Why is it wrong to say one could have such a diary? The temptation is to suppose that there are factual reasons: our language does not work like that; the concepts used in recognizing a sensation are public ones; there would be no independent check on one's memory; and so forth. In short, 'entries in a private diary' cannot be verified. It is easy to approach this section of the 'argument' at such a level.

The sequence of observations concerning sensations makes a different sense if it is seen in the light of the previous section.[6] In that case, it will hardly seem possible that it should be a factual investigation. What else could it be? What objective is in sight?

The 'argument' about private diaries seems to belong with some material later on about 'mental processes.' The grammatical similarity between psychological sentences and external reports might lead one to think of the 'mental theater,' on whose stage these mental objects cavort. Once again, it is a question of eliminating the open space. There is no room between the toothache and the 'Ouch!'; thus the 'Ouch!' is not a report. But the same is true of the other mental processes; they are holistic and not mechanical in nature.[7]

In that case the concern about 'private naming' of a sensation would not be intended to deny the occurrence of any behavior, or indeed the possibility of 'recognizing' one's pains, *in an ordinary sense*. The point would be that the 'private language' use is an extraordinary sense. Once a space is opened up between one's pains and one's recognition of them, an infinite regress becomes possible: ' "Well, I *believe* that this is the sensation S again." – Perhaps you *believe* that you believe it!'[8] The dilemma can only be solved by recognizing that you do not *believe*, in the ordinary sense, that the sensation reappears. Rather, you simply have the same sensation; there is no question about it. The same point is made by Wittgenstein's example of the mental timetable in section 265.

Some light is shed on this material by the following paragraph from the *Investigations*.

> That expression of doubt has no part in the language-game; but if we cut out human behaviour, which is the expression of sensation, it looks as if I might *legitimately* begin to doubt afresh. My temptation to say that one might take a sensation for something other than what it is arises from this: if I assume the abrogation of the normal language-game with the expression of a sensation, I need a criterion of identity for the sensation; and then the possibility of error also exists.[9]

A philosophical problem is arising with the idea of sensation simply because 'language is going on holiday'; one has only to look at the context in order to eliminate the problem.

The necessary complement to the above remark on context can be gleaned from a single sentence found in the very next section of the *Investigations*: 'To use a word without justification does not mean to use it without right.'[10] One might be led to the (mental or physical) 'process' theory of sensation reporting if one were seeking to legitimize pain-utterances. But in ordinary circumstances (in the language-game of sensations) there is no need for such legitimization. The need for explanations has stopped; the individual is for these purposes indivisible. As Wittgenstein points out, an explanation could not be required for every possible problem; the result of such a demand would be the centipede's dilemma.

In the particular case of psychological language, decisions on the need for observations are part of the 'grammar' of the terms. The grammar of first-person present terms is not the same as that of those in the third person: the former do not require observation and do not permit of explanation; the latter do.[11]

This is of course not to say that there are not extraordinary circumstances in which some other proof might be required. There is a language-game of lying; a language-game of play-acting; a language-game of malingering. In some cases we might be unsure just which of these language-games our interlocutor is engaged in. Then the problem is compounded. But these circumstances *are* extraordinary. There are particular surroundings in which we might expect them: a poker game, a theater, the prospect of a hard day's work. Absent these surroundings, there is no reason to assume that things are other than they seem.

A last confusion on this point might arise in connection with the simile of the 'beetle in the box.' If the outside of the box is all that is ever seen publicly, then the supposed contents have 'no place in the language-game at all, not even as a *something*: for the box might even be empty. – No, one can "divide through" by the thing in the box; it cancels out, whatever it is.'[12] Compare *Zettel*, section 550: 'What purpose is served by the statement: "I do *have* something, if I have a pain?"' The aim here is again to show that the deep grammar is different, even though the game played *looks* like one where there is an object or a physical thing I have.

This might be taken for behaviorism. The contents of the person are irrelevant, only her behavior is worthy of note. Wittgenstein's association of words' meaning with use has led some interpreters in this direction. But Wittgenstein is careful to point out that he is rejecting only a grammar, and not a metaphysics.[13] If one understands sensation-talk on the model of 'object' and 'name,' then the 'object' is irrelevant. But whereas the behaviorist does so understand sensation, Wittgenstein does not.[14] 'What greater difference could there be' than between pain-behavior with pain and false pain-behavior, he asks. The individual *does* have internality; but it does not consist of objects which are then reported. He rejects the idea that language only conveys thoughts concerning a variety of internal and external existents.[15] 'The meaning of a word' is often 'its use in the language.' This is not for any positivist, verificationist, or behaviorist reasons; it does not invite factual inquiry. Wittgenstein appeals to use, or usage (*Gebrauch*), where reasons come to an end.[16]

Wittgenstein's disapproval of mechanical explanations is further shown in the *Zettel*, where he discusses psychophysical parallelism. In a way this is an extension of the various arguments against 'having mental objects.' If ideas are things, and they are processed by the brain much as a computer would process them (for instance if human memory is thought of as similar in function to computer memory), then the extreme variety of possible human behaviors and results begins to make the brain look like something 'occult,' as Wittgenstein puts it.

> Thought can as it were *fly*, it doesn't have to walk. You do not understand your own transactions, that is to say you do not have a synoptic view of them, and you as it were project your lack of understanding into the idea of a medium in which the most astounding things are possible.[17]

But if this model is abandoned and thinking regarded as a 'game' similar to, but not exactly the same as computing, then it no longer seems impossible.[18] It is not a question of rejecting subjectivity, but of altering the model on which we base our understanding of it. Wittgenstein's effort in this direction is conceptual and not factual.

Wittgenstein's understanding of the irreplaceable nature and importance of the individual comes to prominence in connection with an important question concerning language-games and 'forms of life': the problem of inter-game understanding and relativism.

As usual with Wittgenstein, there could be various interpretations of the term 'form of life.' (J. F. M. Hunter suggests four possibilities in one article!)[19] There is a continuing debate over the scope of the phenomenon referred to by this term. Both very broad and very narrow interpretations have been offered.[20] Peter Winch has suggested that 'humanity' in general is a form of life.[21] Others have claimed that the only coherent interpretation limits the scope to the social component of individual linguistic practices ('asking, thanking, cursing, greeting, praying' and the like), and that, in fact, 'form of life' and 'language-game' are nearly interchangeable. Recently, Hilmy has attempted to show that a narrow interpretation is correct on the grounds that 'forms of life' must be able to generate or support the meaning of specific signs, and no wide and nebulous phenomenon would have the necessary 'specificity.'[22]

All of these interpretations share the presupposition that when Wittgenstein spoke of 'forms of life,' he was naming a metaphysical entity which he discovered. It is thus very frustrating to find it ill-defined. But this lack of definition may be quite intentional. Rather, there may have been no intent to define at all. As was noted in chapter 2, Wittgenstein only mentions the features of his invented concepts which are necessary to the purpose at hand, leaving them somewhat indeterminate. After all, they are reminders and not metaphysical assertions. Indeed, this indeterminacy is an important part of his methodology, which he explicitly defends in the case of 'language-games.'[23] Nor is it an arbitrary choice or an affectation on his part; the rules of natural languages are always in transition. As he is at some pains to point out, there is no such thing as a rule which fully specifies every application. Every activity, including language use, is an exploration of what the rules allow or suggest.

In keeping with this general observation, it is important to remember that the term 'language-game' is not intended as a systematic category (or worse, a metaphysical assertion about how things must be). It reminds us, not only that language as a human activity is subject to rules, but also that various rules are possible, and that rules may change.

Language-games give general guidelines of the application of language. Wittgenstein suggests that there are innumerably many language-games: innumerably many kinds of use of the components of language.[24] The grammar of the language-game influences the possible relations of words, and things, within that game. But the players may modify the rules gradually. Some utterances within a given language-game are applications; others are 'grammatical remarks' or definitions of what is or should be possible. (Hence Wittgenstein's remark, 'Theology as grammar'[25] – the grammar of religion.)

The idea of the 'form of life' is a reminder about even more basic phenomena. It is clearly bound up with the idea of language. (Language and 'form of life' are explicitly connected in four of the five passages from the *Investigations* in which the term 'form of life' appears.) Just as grammar is subject to change through language-uses, so 'form of life' is subject to change through changes in language. (The Copernican revolution is a paradigm case of this.)

Nevertheless, 'form of life' expresses a deeper level of 'agreement.' It is the level of 'what has to be accepted, the given.'[26] This is an agreement prior to agreement in opinions and decisions. Not everything can be doubted or judged at once.

This suggests that 'form of life' does not denote static phenomena of fixed scope. Rather, it serves to remind us of the general need for context in our activity of meaning. But the context of our meaning is a constantly changing mosaic involving both broad strokes and fine-grained distinctions.

The more commonly understood point of the 'Private Language Argument' – concerning the root of meaning in something public – comes into play here. But it is important to show just what public phenomenon Wittgenstein has in mind. He remarks: 'Only in the stream of thought and life do words have meaning.'[27] But what this does not indicate is a rational or consensual bestowal of meaning. That sort of move could easily be the first step in an infinite regress. For the bestowal would then stand in need of justification. One of Wittgenstein's favorite lines expresses this point perfectly. 'In the beginning was the deed.'[28] Language – discussion – is secondary. This ironic reversal marks him once and for all as something other than a linguistic philosopher! The remarks on 'pain-behavior' have already suggested that it can be profitable to think of language as a particularly complex form of deed.[29] His emphasis is on the context, and not the words.

The idea of 'seeing-as' is clearly germane to the discussion at this point. For the 'form of life' and language-games being instantiated will be strong factors in determining how any object or situation is seen, conceptualized, and understood. But here is where the problem of relativism arises. How can people within one form of life and language-game communicate with those outside their community – much less convert them?

In some situations an artificial answer has been imposed from above: a form of life which both parties share, though they may have disagreements at another level. A good example of this kind of resolution is the system of civil law. But a situation much more difficult to resolve may arise when the conflict is between a religious believer and a non-believer, or between a 'westerner' and a 'primitive.' It is in this last case that some of the most famous battles over the application of Wittgenstein's thought have been waged.

One possible position in this debate is that upheld by Alasdair MacIntyre.[30] He maintains that, in order to escape the specter of relativism, any 'understanding' of another group can only be in the terms of the observer's 'criteria of rationality.' This understanding is to be based on an impartial observation of the empirical facts. The observer will then go on to legitimize or refute the 'rationality of the criteria.' Deviations from the observer's rationality on the part of the observed society are to be explained, partly by the use of historical investigations into their origins.[31] Thus it is possible for the modern western scientist to explain the 'irrelevance' of both Zande and Christian beliefs. Nor can the subjects object to the analysis, unless they wish to be labeled cultural relativists (and dismissed). Thus anyone who 'understands' Christianity cannot believe it; any believer does not understand it.[32]

This analysis leaves one with a feeling of discomfort. Part of the reason for this feeling is that it simply is possible to get from one world view to another. One can imagine a Nuer tribesman going to Oxford, and gaining an 'understanding' of western science and various other belief systems (including his own and Christianity) – then becoming a Christian missionary and returning home. How would MacIntyre explain this series of changes in world view?

One obvious answer is the phenomenon of 'conversion.' The convert learns to 'go on' in a different way from before, seeing a different aspect of the world which presents itself to her. But this is not a complete description of all the possibilities.

A further set of possibilities is suggested by the existence of certain remarkable individuals who seem able to operate in more than one world view, nearly at will. Kierkegaard and Wittgenstein are good examples.[33] It would be hard to dispute that Kierkegaard both 'understood' and 'believed' Christianity. Wittgenstein's understanding of religion is also a far more friendly one than MacIntyre's. MacIntyre provides two more examples, those of E. E. Evans-Pritchard and E. R. Leach. He attributes the remarkable usefulness of their works to the fact that, although their theories are nearly opposite, they do set out their methods and prejudices, then give their reports (which are subject to these prejudices). But this suggests that their grasp of the other culture is separable from their (theoretical) 'understanding' of it. In other words, the *way* in which they understand, yet don't believe, leaves open the possibility that one might both understand and believe.[34]

These few examples are reinforced by the ease with which one slips from one language-game to another within a language and culture. In writing these words, for instance, I am combining facility in philosophy and in the use of the word-processing program I am using. Examples from other games are imported at need. In many cases, two concepts in different games are accessed using the same word. (Compare Wittgenstein's discussion of 'calling to memory,' Kierkegaard's existential concern with memory from *Either/Or*, and my concern that this chapter not grow too large to fit into my computer's memory.) Difficulties in accomplishing this function are the exception, rather than the rule. They are often funny, like the Looking-Glass discussion of Nobody.

This circuitous discussion is now ready to return to one of its starting points – the importance of the individual in Wittgenstein's thought. Several examples will serve to show this importance. How do examples from music come to the service of philosophy? Wittgenstein uses them, and his readers must participate in both games to get his point. How is it that anti-Hegelian metaphysics comes to the service of religious commitment? Kierkegaard relates them. How is it that Gorbachev and Reagan communicate? A translator interposes himself. How is it that the link between language-games is made? I make it.

Each of these examples stresses the point, often made by Wittgenstein, that language-games are *activities* (just as philosophy is an activity). In fact, 'the term "language-*game*" is meant to bring into prominence the fact that the *speaking* of language is part of an activity, or of a form of life.'[35] The primary feature is that 'this language-game is played' – *not* that 'the rules of this language-game exist.' A great danger of metaphors such as 'language-game' and 'seeing-as' is that they will be understood to suggest subliminal processes in which actions are chosen by mentally 'looking up' rules, or objects recognized through comparison with a checklist of features such as computer 'perception' uses. It is the action of playing which is basic, and not a proto-metaphysical framework of rules.[36] This is an extension of the claim that 'in the beginning was the deed.' The active element of application is essential to the very nature of rules, as Wittgenstein's comments on 'going on' also claim to show.

For this reason, any attempt to treat various cultures or societies as scientific systems (that is, static sets of rules) is doomed to create misunderstandings at the least. In reality, the 'rules' are subject to constant reinterpretation. Compare Kierkegaard's dictum: 'An existential system is impossible.' It is impossible partly because no codification can take all future possibilities into account. How future events will be related to the system is necessarily a matter for on-the-spot interpretation.[37]

A most important consequence of the examples above is that the playing of (one or more) games is only possible for *people*, not for theories. If various societies cannot be understood on the model of 'Hegelian' static systems, but must be understood as active and organic wholes (which at some level are not rule-governed but rule-interpretive), then the obvious point of connection and comparison between them is the individual. Deeds require doers.[38] Only the individual 'player' can provide a connection between games without the need for a meta-system which describes and classifies all games. There is a large variety of ways in which we do in fact participate in more than one game. Some were mentioned above. Consider also: a chess player playing several games at once; an actor, in character, 'playing' chess in a play; the chess game in *Through the Looking-Glass*, a novel created by Lewis Carroll (himself created by Charles Dodgson!), and in which the pieces have personalities and are characters in a story. After these examples, the work of the simultaneous translator or the anthropologist no longer seems so unusual – which is not to say that it is less extraordinary – and the one-way trip of the religious convert begins to seem simplistic![39]

In the foregoing we have traced through one problem, in an attempt to show how some interpretations of Wittgenstein's method can lead to difficulties in grasping his intentions, and the breadth of phenomena in which he was interested. We began with one heuristic device: the discussion of internal dialogues, as an example of the rejected notion 'mental process.' This device has been reified into an 'argument.' When the argument is applied systematically, it casts great doubt on Wittgenstein's appreciation for the individual. And his stress on such social phenomena as 'language-games' can easily be taken as additional evidence of this disdain. But in following Wittgenstein's own method – applying his tools to a problem, namely that of the possibility of connections between language-games or forms of life – we have seen that the individual has great importance in playing and working out these games. Only when they are conceived as structured systems in which the individual is trapped do problems of relativism arise. *Existing* individuals feel no such bonds. To try to explain why they don't, do, or should is not appropriate – it is not a matter for explanation, but for some other kind of grasping. As Wittgenstein remarks, 'I act with *complete* certainty. But this certainty is my own.'[40] The deed is foundational, and only individuals are capable of deeds.

A systematic answer to the question 'Is understanding religion compatible with believing?' is also at the root of a common misunderstanding of Kierkegaard's thought. Yet in this case the problem is turned upside-down. For while applying 'system' to Wittgenstein seems to make the individual subject disappear, in the case of Kierkegaard it is the social dimension which 'vanishes' in his concern with subjectivity, once again leaving the claim of total relativism. The stress on the subjective also leads to the suggestion of irrationalism.

What makes Kierkegaard particularly interesting in the context of the discussion of 'forms of life' is that he gives remarkable literary evocations of several different ways of life or language-games. The scheme of the 'stages' or 'spheres' of existence, first seen in *Either/Or*, is taken up again in *Stages on Life's Way* and used as well in the *Postscript*. There can be no disputing that his grasp of these stages is complete – the best witness to this being that the 'Diary of the Seducer,' one of the aesthetic sections of *Either/Or*, has been published separately as a serious aesthetic work.[41] While this is a great compliment to Kierkegaard's skill, it is difficult to imagine a more absurd abstraction from context.

Interpretations of Kierkegaard's thought which begin from the assumption that he is a 'systematic' philosopher are far more common. One type of interpretation thinks of the stages as a fixed, almost metaphysical hierarchy.[42] Another takes the idea of paradox and 'irrationality' as paradigmatic of Kierkegaard's thought (or at least of his writings) and reacts to this idea.

A particularly useful facet of Kierkegaard's thought in the unravelling of these conflicting claims is his interest in the transitions between stages of existence, language-games, and ways of thinking. Most of the interpretations center on static features of his work, but his own method and goals were dynamic; the method was pointing, and pointing toward becoming rather than being.[43]

The place of the philosophically oriented pseudonymous writings (particularly the *Fragments* and *Postscript*), and the weight to be given to the 'theses' contained in them, is a disputed point. One particular school of thought is concerned to save Kierkegaard from himself. For instance, Henry Allison's strategy is to show that if Kierkegaard's 'Climacus' works really mean what they appear to say, then Kierkegaard would indeed be an irrationalist; hence it is 'obvious' that they are a peculiar and one-dimensional kind of indirect communication – parodies of serious Hegelianism.[44] This interpretation is also supported by Alistair McKinnon's word-frequency studies, which show that use of the term 'paradox' is limited to the pseudonymous works. His conclusion is that the category was not Kierkegaard's.[45]

Some of this confusion can be resolved by a clarification of Kierkegaard's understanding of the relative importance of logical understanding as against belief 'by virtue of the absurd.' An important part of his position is summed up this way:

> Nonsense therefore he [the Christian] cannot believe against the understanding, for precisely the understanding will discern that it is nonsense and will prevent him from believing it; but he makes so much use of the understanding that he becomes aware of the incomprehensible, and then he holds to this, believing against the understanding.[46]

He contrasts this position with one which refutes accusations 'by remarking that it is a higher understanding.' That distinction is designed to fend off the Hegelian imperialization of religion by reason. But it also might serve as a response to charges of fideism.

It is clear that one of the most important of the various tools to be used in 'becoming Christian' is the ordinary kind of rationality. This rationality is perfectly capable of dealing with statements which abuse everyday language while pretending to be part of it, such as 'One equals three' or 'The moon is made of green cheese.' To each of these our reply might well be 'Nonsense!'[47] But no one is comfortable with such a reply when confronted with a statement like 'God is three persons in one' or the Australian Aborigine's 'The sun is a white cockatoo.' These smack of the 'incomprehensible.'

Kierkegaard clearly does not disdain rational thought. But another part of his analysis probes the limits of this 'everyday rationality' which the believer uses to distinguish nonsense from the incomprehensible. The problem is set up in terms borrowed from Lessing, who noted that 'accidental historical truths can never serve as proofs for eternal truths of the reason; and that the transition by which it is proposed to base an eternal truth upon historical testimony is a leap.'[48] Kierkegaard provides conceptual support for this claim by an examination of the categories 'possibility,' 'actuality,' and 'necessity.' When historical events 'come into existence,' they go from the category of possibility to that of actuality. But necessity is a separate category: necessary things are eternal existents. The upshot of this discussion is that historical events are merely immutable; they have certainly happened but not happened certainly. In order to base reasoned understandings on them, it is necessary to *appropriate* them. He certainly does not wish to deny that we do appropriate them, but he does wish to point out that historical knowledge is not 'well-founded' in a strictly logical sense of the term. What is 'objectively uncertain' is 'for faith most certain.' The subjective thinker *sees it as* certain. In Wittgenstein's terms, 'this certainty is [his] own.'[49]

There is, however, a sense in which the *Postscript* has to do with Hegelianism. This sense relates to the idea of the 'stages' as a system. Kierkegaard's disdain for 'system' of the Hegelian type is proverbial; it would be astonishing if the stages he discusses were to form such a system.

It would be much easier to think of them under the category of heuristic (or 'maieutic') devices. What better way to 'find the reader where he is' than by showing him how he looks in a mirror! Then it will be possible to show the consequences of the reader's choices in accelerated fashion, and perhaps even to make him change his mind about those choices.

If the only existence-categories to be used are the three stages from the *Stages*, this heuristic scheme might not be effective for everyone. It just seems wrong to suggest that there are in the world only aesthetes, ethicists, and religious persons. Furthermore, for the project to be effective, the subjects to be 'helped' must understand themselves in the way suggested. In that case, at least one more category must be proposed. In Kierkegaard's day of popular Hegelianism (and how much more in the era of 'secular humanism') there were many who saw themselves under another description: as men of reason, thinkers, even philosophers. What better way to communicate the idea of 'becoming a Christian' to these persons, than by presenting an argument which begins in reason, yet eventually shows reason's limits from inside.[50] In that case the *Postscript* would not be a parody of Hegel, but a serious piece of philosophy, albeit with an ulterior, non-philosophical motive.[51] Kierkegaard might also be forgiven in that case for using terms (such as 'paradox') which cast the problem in philosophical language. His failure to use them elsewhere need not indicate a repudiation, but merely the playing of a different language-game.[52]

This understanding of the 'stages' parallels the suggestion made above concerning Wittgenstein's 'forms of life.' In fact, Kierkegaard's fully evolved maieutic project makes the application of Wittgenstein's ideas clear in a way which philosophical discussion cannot.

It might be pointed out (for example, by Alasdair MacIntyre) that for all Kierkegaard's insistence on the ultimate necessity for the Christian faith, nevertheless he shows no 'understanding' of it. In fact, he does not show even a grasp of it, at least in terms which those not possessed of the Christian perspective can understand. MacIntyre could say that this lack of objective rational criteria leaves Kierkegaard without a foothold from which to differentiate the form of life he recommends, let alone any arguments for adopting it. How can it be that he really has something to recommend?[53]

An answer to this question might be formulated along the lines of Wittgenstein's discussion of rule-following and the continuation of series. Part of the response rests on Kierkegaard's understanding of the essential importance of situation; this has ramifications distinctly similar to those of Wittgenstein's category of deed. Kierkegaard agrees that 'how a saying [*ein Wort*] is understood is not told by words alone.'[54] He notes that

> all speaking with the mouth is a kind of ventriloquism, an indeterminate something. The deception is that there is, after all, a definite visible figure who uses his mouth. But take care. Language is an abstraction.
>
> In order for speaking actually to become human speech in a deeper sense, or in a spiritual sense, something else is required

> with respect to being the one who speaks, two points must be determined: the one is the speech, the words spoken, the other is the situation.
>
> The situation determines decisively whether or not the speaker is in character with what he says, or the situation determines whether or not the words are spoken at random, a talking which is unattached.⁵⁵

Thus 'Christendom' is pictured as a kind of ventriloquists' convention, in which unappropriated statements of a religious kind are in the air. In this context, Christians can be known by the earnestness of their expression. Words said on Sunday must show their application during the week. The 'spy' of the *Postscript* seeks out examples of the ironical lack of such application in Christendom.

Kierkegaard accents this visible side of Christianity at many points in his acknowledged works. The idea central to the expression of earnestness is *imitation* of Christ. 'Imitation must be introduced, to exert pressure in the direction of humility. It is to be done quite simply in this way: Everyone must be measured by the Pattern, the ideal.'⁵⁶ The danger – the actual event in Christendom – is that imitation is left to the 'extraordinary' person (for example, the medieval monastic), and is no longer required of all followers.⁵⁷ But it is only this imitation that can distinguish Christianity from verbally similar mythology or poetry.⁵⁸

It is significant that in speaking of Abraham and Job, Kierkegaard does not stress their words. Instead, he discusses and describes their actions. It is true that in the case of Job, he begins with a saying: 'The Lord gave, and the Lord hath taken away; blessed be the name of the Lord.' 'But the expression itself is not the guidance, and Job's significance does not lie in the fact that he said it, but in the fact that he acted in accordance with it.'⁵⁹ What is important about this saying is not its intrinsic richness as a doctrine – if it were, then the words might be remembered, but Job would be long forgotten – but instead Job's life as 'pattern for succeeding generations.'

The importance of conforming actions to words is stressed in a variety of other edifying discourses. The most explicit of these is based on a passage from the Epistle of James: 'But be doers of the word, and not hearers only, deceiving yourselves.'⁶⁰ Kierkegaard remarks that 'every verbal expression is very imperfect, compared with the precision of performance.'[61] The meaning of the Word is shown in the use to which it is put.

It might seem sufficient merely to name another of Kierkegaard's discourses, *Works of Love*. The title already suggests an external qualification of Christianity. This might appear to be at odds with Kierkegaard's demand for inwardness. But he rejects the idea that inwardness can properly be hidden.[62] *Works of Love* explores the intricate dialectic between the inward and the outward qualifications of love's work. The tension inherent in this dialectic is made plain in the first section, on 'love's hidden life and its recognizability by its fruits.'

Kierkegaard begins by reaffirming the essentially hidden nature of the root of love. God's love is the mysterious spring of human love.[63] Kierkegaard decries the 'conceited shrewdness' of positivism, which denies the unseen, and only cheats itself of the richness of life.[64] In any case, a little patience will reveal an outward expression. The hidden root is to be known by its fruits. There is something to be seen!

But Kierkegaard protests against the 'miserable mistrust' which insists on seeing *others*' fruits. The saying that love is to be 'recognizable' is not a claim about verification, but an exhortation to be fruitful. It is a grammatical rather than a factual remark. Love's grammar differs from that of positivism; it is charitable (a work of love) to believe the best about others without demanding evidence.[65] 'Love's recognizability' does not imply looking at others to judge their fruits, but looking to oneself in concern over one's own fruits. To undergo this change in outlook would be a true fruit of love.

The relation between words and deeds is again addressed in the section on love as 'the fulfilling of the law.' Kierkegaard takes up a Gospel parable on the subject of promising. One brother says 'I go, sir,' but does not; the other says 'I will not,' but finally goes. The danger lies in assuming that a performative utterance is the whole performance; promising is after all a mere engagement. The fulfillment of this word in deeds is more important. Love is known by the deeds it engenders.[66]

Kierkegaard finds a rigorous demand for action even in the apparently mild statement, 'Be it done for you as you have believed.' On the face of it, this saying does not impose any external standard of judgement on the individual, let alone a standard of action. But it is the test of the action. Certainly, it cannot serve as a standard for the judgement of others. It is *one's own* actions that must conform to this demand.[67]

All of this could be considered as an extended grammatical reflection on the status of Christendom and Christianity. Everyone knows the words. But how are they to be understood? Only one's actions can show how they have in fact been understood. The meaning of the word is shown by its usage, the inward work of love by its fruits.[68]

This teleological qualification of Kierkegaard's understanding of Christianity – a demand for outwardness – is powerful ammunition against the charge of subjectivism.[69]

Another part of the answer to MacIntyre's question involves a reminder about Kierkegaard's purpose. It must be pointed out once again that Kierkegaard's concern is the problem of 'becoming a Christian.' His specific method is to present the problem of becoming a Christian in such a way that his audience sees the necessity for this problem to be solved. It is not up to him to give a complete and anthropologically sound description of the Christian life.

But indeed there is no reason why he should be able to give such a description to his intended audience. He is trying to lead them to the point where they are living this description for themselves. He is not giving objective content, but at most pointing out the way to continue in a certain game. As Wittgenstein's remarks on rule-following suggest, this teaching is an uncertain business. What it is to become a Christian – the direction to be followed – may be pointed out. What it is to become a Christian, the experience of following that path, is forever hidden from those who have not themselves followed it. Johannes de Silentio, the author of *Fear and Trembling*, reports: 'Abraham I cannot understand, in a certain sense I can learn nothing from him except to be amazed.'[70] Yet he has shown the possibilities inherent in Abraham's situation and decision as well as they can be rationally presented.

Kierkegaard presents a theoretical justification for his method in the *Postscript*: 'Dialectics itself does not see the absolute, but it leads, as it were, the individual up to it, and says: "Here it must be, that I guarantee; when you worship here you worship God."'[71]

The beginning of a response to this final send-off is: 'Now I can go on'. Dialectical explanations come to an end sometime: there can only be the exasperated repetition of the prolegomena. What is particularly astonishing about Kierkegaard – and about Wittgenstein and other thinkers who have been able themselves to bridge the gap between language-games of especially wide separation – is the tremendous breadth and depth of attempts they make to lead others to the point of grasping the essential.[72] But, in a simile reminiscent of that other Johannes Climacus, Wittgenstein says:

> My propositions serve as elucidations in the following way: Anyone who understands me eventually recognizes them as nonsensical, when he has used them – as steps – to climb up beyond them. (He must, so to speak, throw away the ladder after he has climbed up it.)
>
> He must transcend these propositions, and then he will see the world aright.[73]

Kierkegaard and Wittgenstein have different ends in view. Wittgenstein is concerned to show the way out of theoretical muddles related to the structure of the way we see the world. Kierkegaard is concerned to show the way between two ways of viewing the world. A possibility largely latent in Wittgenstein's work, that there may be many *prima facie* self-consistent ways of seeing the world, is taken for granted as the basis of Kierkegaard's whole project.

One aspect which ties the applications of their methods together is a very high regard for the individual in his subjectivity. Problems which appear insoluble when they are set up as metaphysical situations in need of theory-laden 'interpretation' are handled as matters of routine by the existing individual. Only with an appreciation for this occurrence can either author's points be grasped.

The importance of the individual is likely to be forgotten in Wittgenstein's stress on the social categories of deed, language, and form of life. There is an equal danger that external aspects may be forgotten in Kierkegaard's stress on the individual's subjectivity. But both authors would agree that both aspects are necessary; for there to be appropriation, some*one* must appropriate some*thing*.

The maieutic method which both authors use and approve clearly demonstrates this connection of individual and social. To ask an individual to see things differently presupposes both the existence of communities of thought and the individual's freedom to move between them. If anything in their work can be 'applied' in an extension of this work, such a method must surely be part of that extension. It is fitting that a tool, rather than a theory, is to be applied.

In Kierkegaard's writings the application of the regard for the individual has a clearer directionality. Everything the reader is invited to notice is pointed in one direction, that is, toward Christianity.

Wittgenstein also has something to say about the field of religion, however. The next chapter will explore how Wittgenstein's and Kierkegaard's way of working can contribute to the study and 'understanding' of (and not merely conversion to) religion. In the course of this discussion the questions of 'fideism' and 'relativism' will be addressed more explicitly.

Chapter Four

IMPLICATIONS FOR RELIGION

No investigation of the positions of Kierkegaard and Wittgenstein on the subject of religion can escape their fundamental asymmetry on one point: Kierkegaard was 'a religious writer,' and Wittgenstein was not. But this bald assertion about the two authors' ultimate concerns is likely to come in for important qualifications when the authorships are examined in detail.

The most obvious evidence in this case is the amount of written material devoted to the subject. On this basis the first suggestion holds true. The vast majority of Kierkegaard's work has something to do with religion, although he did publish pseudonymously some works that could be taken for novels and even literary criticism.

Wittgenstein, on the other hand, made public very little material which has a *prima facie* connection with religious issues. He gave one short paper, the 'Lecture on Ethics.' He also spoke about religious belief in a course given around the year 1938; student notes from these sessions have been published. In the manuscripts which he himself published or edited for publication, there are only a few references to religion. These include the remarks on the 'ethical' and 'mystical' at the end of the *Tractatus*, and scattered comments on 'theology as grammar' in the *Investigations*, *Zettel*, and other later works. Some notes culled from manuscripts on other topics have been posthumously collected as *Culture and Value*; this is a small volume, and by no means all of it is concerned with religion.[1]

Kierkegaard's ideas about authorship and the author's 'task' are germane at this point. His report on his 'point of view' gives a synoptic understanding of his works, including the ones which are not overtly religious in tone. As evidence for the appropriateness of this understanding he proposes his perception of his own religious situation. Thus he is able to claim that he did not *develop* into a religious writer; he was always one, and the apparently non-religious works will be understood as religious when they are seen in context.

Wittgenstein also understood there to be a connection between his life and his works. This understanding has been sketched out in chapter 1. It is apparent from his biography that he had a deep personal interest in religion. Thus, in trying to decide how to apply Wittgenstein's ideas to religion, it is necessary to take into account his overall attitude toward religious phenomena; a mere counting of occasions on which they are mentioned is not enough.

Wittgenstein's self-understanding suggests that his few remarks about religion deserve to be taken seriously. But there are so few of them that not much can be made of them alone. What is more interesting is that these remarks clearly follow from the way of thinking evident in his philosophical work in general. They suggest a line along which a religious investigation might be continued.

Kierkegaard sets forward the idea that *what* is sought can find its expression in *how* it is sought. He limits the use of this idea to one specific occasion: the subjectivity of faith. Near the end of the *Postscript*, he remarks that the '*how* of the Christian' can only correspond with the absolute paradox.[2] Thus maximal subjectivity becomes objectively unique.[3] In the pseudonymous literature, Kierkegaard makes considerable play from the compatibility of his subjective position (partially understood) with various basic concerns. But *The Point of View* suggests a particular understanding of how he has worked. Only in the light of this understanding can the overall 'what' – the point of his authorship – become clear. When the unity of his work is understood, then his aesthetic and philosophical writings can show their fullest implications.

One of Wittgenstein's sayings suggests a more general use of this method. In discussing the nature of mathematical proof, he remarks: 'Tell me *how* you seek and I will tell you *what* you are seeking.'[4] What makes the application of this suggestion more difficult in this particular case is the complex nature of Wittgenstein's methods. Discovering just how he is working is itself a major task, some part of which has been attempted in earlier chapters.[5]

IMPLICATIONS FOR RELIGION

To obtain an 'objective' idea of Wittgenstein's position on religion, one would need to bear in mind his methodology and its application in general, as well as his personal interest in religion. One aspect of his methodology which will bear special watching is the appeal to the individual. Any points of unity between the earlier and later works would also be a great help.

Wittgenstein's attitude toward religion (or the type of problems for which religion is commonly a solution) is most plainly illustrated in his understanding of the *Tractatus*. That understanding has its clearest expression in Wittgenstein's letter to Ficker.[6] There he claims that 'the sense of the book is an ethical one,' and what is important is what is *not* written. Furthermore (according to the preface of the book itself) the value of the work is partly that it shows how little is achieved when the problems of philosophy are definitively solved.[7]

What remains to be achieved beyond the solution of specific problems of philosophy is the attribution of a sense to the world. This might be a response to the experience of 'wondering at the existence of the world'; it might take the form of 'feeling *absolutely* safe.'[8]

The need to impose some order on the world is also a driving force in Kierkegaard's existential dialectic. One way in which this need is expressed is as 'anxiety.' Such anxiety is not an 'imperfection,' but rather a necessary first step. This feeling of heterogeneity is a function of the human freedom which makes Christian progress toward perfection possible.[9] Kierkegaard's concern with the 'maieutic' and the category 'becoming' is partly an attempt to cause anxiety, or recognition of anxiety, in his readers. This reflects an interesting difference between his task and Wittgenstein's. For Wittgenstein, anxiety is already present in philosophy; the correct vision may alleviate it. (It is only in the task of redefining philosophy – Wittgenstein's more-or-less permanent methodological contribution – that he must first shake his readers loose from their pre-existing concepts.) But for Kierkegaard it is first necessary to create anxiety in order fruitfully to suggest the direction of Christianity.

Wittgenstein's personal feelings of inadequacy could easily be understood as an example of the kind of anxiety suggested above. But while he discusses what resolutions of philosophical anxiety would be like, it is not immediately clear what would count as a resolution of his more personal, more ethical anxiety.

A distinguishing feature of all the suggestions for easing anxiety made above is that they do not have to do with any 'propositions' or descriptions of how things are in the world. 'Wondering at the existence of the world' is not like astonishment at the size of that Great Dane. The dog's size might be explained by facts concerning its breeding and diet. Such factual explanations are not available concerning the 'riddle of life.' Thus skepticism is as much a category-mistake as metaphysics – it tries to raise factual doubts where conceptual problems are encountered.[10] Wittgenstein goes so far as to say that he would reject any attempt to explain religion as factually significant just because of the dimension in which the explanation is attempted.[11] The 'riddle of life' is an existential problem; facts are not transparently at issue.

Kierkegaard's analysis of anxiety as a function of infinite possibilities (and the subject's realization that the possibilities are indeed infinite) trades on a similar understanding. Faith's role in bringing a practical halt to the possibilities recalls the more secular role of belief in assenting to historical facts.[12] Anxiety takes a piecemeal approach to the factual possibilities, just as the skeptical attitude toward historical belief points out the various points where a 'proof' could theoretically be demanded. When anxiety or doubt is annulled, it is not merely a question of asserting one particular fact, but instead depends on a more profound change of the individual's attitude toward possibility. In Kierkegaard's explication, Abraham's actions – in a situation which could never be factually reconciled – are paradigmatic of the faithful attitude.

Wittgenstein's call for an end to explanations mirrors Kierkegaard's analysis of the historical. And Wittgenstein too sees a relation between 'historical' or everyday belief and the religious. In the *Tractatus*, Wittgenstein calls both logic and ethics 'transcendental.' That is, neither deals with facts on the propositional level. But he suffers from the straitjacket of the attempt to explain language by the picture theory, with its attendant metaphysics. Since all language is propositional, logic (which underlies language, tying it to what is the case) and ethics (which lies beyond language and alterations in what is the case) are permanently separated. Language is 'a cage' which resists attempts to talk significantly about things outside the factual realm. Still, the thrust of this tendency '*points to something.*'[13]

Wittgenstein's analysis of this separation in the earlier works turns on a particular understanding of the possibilities of language. This understanding is mirrored in the structure of the *Tractatus*. Its numbered propositional form serves as a ladder. Yet the purpose of this ladder is not ascent. Rather, it is to be '*trans*cended.'

The *Tractatus* conception of the 'mystical' is connected with Wittgenstein's understanding of the self as transcendent. Only something outside the world can have a full view of it. The self marks the limit of the world. The world is mirrored in language. The self's transcendence of language implies a transcendence of the world, and the possibility of new understanding not bound by language.

A passage from the *Investigations* suggests a possible re-evaluation of this 'transcendence' of language.

> To say 'this combination of words makes no sense' excludes it from the sphere of language and thereby bounds the domain of language. But when one draws a boundary it may be for various kinds of reason. If I surround an area with a fence or a line or otherwise, the purpose may be to prevent someone from getting in or out; but it may also be part of a game and the players be supposed, say, to jump over the boundary; or it may shew where the property of one man ends and that of another begins; and so on. So if I draw a boundary that is not yet to say what I am drawing it for.[14]

At the time of the 'Lecture of Ethics' Wittgenstein did not remark this feature of boundaries. There he speaks of the border as having only one side. He explains the function of religious language as akin to that of simile. But he claims that the 'ethical' use of language is informed by a 'characteristic misuse.'[15]

A simile is an explanation of one structure by means of another. That other thing ought in principle to be describable in its own terms. For example, one might describe a tapestry as a rug hung like a picture. This description would make clear both the appearance and the construction of the tapestry. But it would also be possible to give a description in terms of the mechanics of design and weaving. This kind of description would be 'more fully analyzed.'

In the case of religion and ethics, however, the object of the simile is not describable otherwise than by the simile. Nor is this a contingent fact which is subject to remedy by further scientific investigation; rather the 'simile' is in this case an attempt to use language to express something beyond the linguistically definable world. Insofar as ethics and religion are attempts to get beyond language, they are 'hopeless': they will never be scientific.

It would be possible to understand Kierkegaard's 'leap' to a 'perspective of faith' in these categories as well. Abraham was involved in a 'teleological suspension of the ethical.' If this were the complete story, the basis of the charge of 'fideism' would be reasonably clear. If religion operates beyond the limits of the definable world (in a 'suspension of the logical'), then it is necessarily inaccessible to reason. But the idea of multiple 'stages' suggests that a more complex analysis is required.

Wittgenstein's later thought is at odds with the metaphor of language as a cage. In fact, an important change in Wittgenstein's thinking seems to have occurred between December 1929 and December 1930. Two conversations held in those months are recorded. In the earlier conversation (and in the 'Lecture on Ethics' of about the same date), he expands on the idea of the cage, comparing it with Kierkegaard's category of paradox. But in the later conversation he rejects the whole conception. Instead he remarks that 'the essence of religion can have nothing to do with whether speech occurs – or rather: if speech does occur, this itself is a component of religious behavior and not a theory.'[16] If language is not essential to a 'definition' of religion, then the possibility of religion could hardly be bounded by the inability to formulate a theory. Speech which is a *component* of religion suggests the idea of the primacy of activity explicated in the previous chapter. The roots of the religious game might indeed be inexpressible in scientific terms, just as the roots of science are, without religious life being inconsistent or ineffable.

It is interesting to note that the idea of 'running up against the limits of language' reappears in the *Investigations*, albeit in a different sense. Philosophy is said to discover the 'bumps' which the understanding has got by running up against the limits of language. But here what the understanding was searching for was a (propositional) meta-understanding or theory, and not a transcendental understanding in the ethical sense.[17] Insofar as reason encounters barriers to its theorizing, the category of paradox is intact, at least in one sense.

In fact this understanding of the problems of reason is

reminiscent in form and implications of the collision between reason and the 'thing that thought cannot think' which Kierkegaard mentions in the *Fragments*. This is also a case of the propositional understanding attempting to assimilate the unassimilable.

If the *Tractatus* were recast in terms of the later categories, then the idea that logic and ethics are 'transcendental' might be translated into the assertion that they are grammatical fields. They 'tell what kind of object anything is.'[18] These grammars are not explicitly laid out a priori, but they can be gathered from the ordinary uses of language.

One part of Kierkegaard's and Wittgenstein's task is the attempt to lay out some of what they have gathered about the grammar of their fields of interest. Some of these presentations relate to the place of the religious.

Various suggestions from the *Investigations* show how 'grammar' might take over the position filled by 'logic' in the *Tractatus*. 'Grammar tells what kind of object anything is'; '*Essence* is expressed by grammar.'[19] (To the first of these remarks Wittgenstein appends the parenthetical remark 'Theology as grammar.') Whereas in the *Tractatus* there is only one grammar and attempts to get beyond it can only end in hopeless running against a wall, in the context of the later works there are multiple available grammars. Wittgenstein even provides an example of a piece of theological grammar: 'You can't hear God speak to someone else, you can hear him only if you are being addressed.'[20] Here the ordinary category 'speech' is modified in the grammar of religion. Whereas anyone within earshot can hear an ordinary speech, God's speeches are quite different. This statement shows part of the framework of a particular kind of religious belief. It might be a reminder, or an attempt to redefine the concepts involved. One can even imagine it being used as a purely factual statement (in a catechetical situation, for instance). At any rate it has a constructive grammatical connotation.

Wittgenstein's statements on the mystical in the *Tractatus* and the 'Lecture on Ethics' can also be construed as 'grammatical.'[21] He is talking of mystical experience, but at the same time bounding the use of the word. No factual content can be ascribed to a 'mystical' experience. The mystical is not within the world nor is its expression within language; instead it shows itself in the existence of the world and the existence of language.[22] This showing can only be felt.[23]

IMPLICATIONS FOR RELIGION

Kierkegaard is performing a grammatical task in his 'Book on Adler.' One of the constant themes of this work is that Adler is confused about the sources of his understanding. First he says that he has received a cleansing revelation, and consequently has burned all of his Hegelian treatises. As Kierkegaard remarks, this implies that he is 'an essential author,' one whose works (like Kierkegaard's) are grounded in his existence.[24] But then he publishes some sermons from before the time of the revelation. Some of these are said to be partially under the influence of the Spirit. Later still, under the cross-examination of the Church, he allows less and less scope to revelation, and more to his own working-out. Now he has descended in Kierkegaard's view to the level of the 'premise-author,' who may have a different premise for each book.[25]

What Kierkegaard finds particularly ridiculous about Adler (and contrary to the spirit of Christianity, to say the least)[26] is that he is unclear about the distinction between genius and special revelation. He could have maintained a modicum of authority and dignity if he had stuck to the idea of revelation.[27] In effect Kierkegaard accuses Adler of making a category-mistake – assuming that genius and revelation have enough in common to be combined (or even mistaken for each other). The clouds of Adler's confusion on this point are condensed into a drop of grammar; this is explicated in Kierkegaard's definition of authority as a *qualitative* difference, quite independent of the content of a message.

Furthermore there is an ethical component to the definition of the essential author. If nothing else, revelation confers an ethical requirement. In confusing revelation and genius, Adler fails in this ethical responsibility. Once authority is claimed, one cannot escape it; this is again a grammatical point.

Kierkegaard's reminder is both theoretical and practical. It distances Kierkegaard from Adler (whose projects might at first glance look similar). Kierkegaard is undoubtedly an essential author, though not one with authority. But he does not shirk the ethical dimension of his task.

Another grammatical idea in the *Tractatus* which relates to the later philosophy is that ethics and aesthetics are the same.[28] (In the 'Lecture on Ethics' Wittgenstein repeats this assertion.) One similarity is that both are kinds of judgement which do not modify anything at the level of fact or proposition, but only something 'higher' or out of the realm of propositions, that is, something 'transcendental.' But it is difficult to understand Wittgenstein's assertion that they are not merely similar, but actually the same.

A possible clue to an understanding is the obvious resemblance between this 'aesthetic' conception of ethics and the later material on 'seeing.' When the duck-rabbit is seen alternately under each of its aspects, nothing propositional has changed. The diagram serves as a proposition; the interpretation is external to it.

In the same way one object may elicit different aesthetic judgements. These do not depend on a change in the propositional description of the object; it is merely evaluated (seen) in different ways.

To say that 'ethics and aesthetics are one and the same' suggests a further extension of this process. The clear pattern of aesthetics is offered as a paradigm for ethics. Wittgenstein reminds us that when varying ethical judgements are made, propositional facts are not usually at the center of the dispute. The interpretation of these facts, or how they are seen, is crucial.

Wittgenstein makes yet another extension of the concepts involved here when he makes 'wonder at the world' an expression of ethics. This suggests not merely a series of disconnected decisions on ethical issues, but a whole way of living, unified in some sense by a quasi-aesthetic understanding of the facts.

Wittgenstein's remarks on color are illuminating here. He discusses the phenomena of contextuality as they apply to the painter's choice of pigment. He remarks on the difficulty in saying exactly what color-impression certain particular patches of paintings give – for instance, the iris of an eye.[29] As he notes, although there is such a thing as gold paint, Rembrandt did not use it in painting *The golden helmet*.[30]

So the understanding of ethics as 'the same' as aesthetics is not idiosyncratic, but a forerunner of Wittgenstein's later understanding of the phenomena of contextuality. He is remarking (proposing?) a grammatical similarity between the two fields.

This understanding of ethics is echoed by Kierkegaard's analysis in *Either/Or* of the inadequacy in the traditional 'ethical' life of Judge William. His duty-based ethics are doomed to failure because, as an existing individual, he will be unable to satisfy the absolute standard on a case-by-case basis. This is made abundantly clear by the sermon included at the end of the work, which

IMPLICATIONS FOR RELIGION

explicates the edification in the idea that 'in relation to God we are always in the wrong.' The ethicist thinks in terms of individual duties. But the infinite multiplicity of these duties must overwhelm him in anxiety. The only possible salvation from this wave of duties is a shift in perspective. The endless stream of duties can only be faced with faith's 'inner certainty.'[31]

When the ethical is removed from the propositional realm, the possible consequences of an ethical decision seem to be removed from this realm as well. Ethical laws in the traditional sense clearly presuppose (or at least strongly suggest) rewards and punishments. But if ethics is not within the world, it would be odd for its consequences to be in the world. If there are to be consequences of good or bad ethical willing, they will not be propositionally expressible.[32] (A conceptual problem with a conceptual solution will surely have conceptual consequences.)

What kind of non-factual effect could ethical willing have? Wittgenstein speaks of the world 'waxing and waning as a whole,' but another phrase he uses is more accessible. 'The world of the happy man is a different one from that of the unhappy man.'[33] This idea connects with the aesthetic view of ethics (and thus with the later material). The happy man sees the world under a different aspect from the unhappy man. This need not suggest any complete doctrinal understanding, merely that clarity which comes with complete disappearance of the problems.[34] This disappearance is not piecemeal answering, but vanishing of life's problems.[35] The answer makes itself manifest (*zeigt sich*). This understanding of the world in its totality is what Wittgenstein calls the 'mystical.'

This conception of the difference between the happy and the unhappy man is given substance in Kierkegaard's description of the difference between the 'Knight of Faith' and the ordinary person. In *Fear and Trembling*, Kierkegaard recounts a meeting with the perfect Knight of Faith. 'Good lord, is this the man, is this really the one – he looks just like a tax-collector!'[36] There is no temporal indication that this might be a particularly religious person, no propositional difference. But the Knight of Faith has a personal confidence. He is ready to partake of the world at its fullest – a fine meal, or even a capitalistic scheme – but if these possibilities should fall through, it will be quite the same to him. His is the world of the happy man, and whatever the accidental facts of his life he remains a happy man. He views the world from a 'perspective of faith.'

IMPLICATIONS FOR RELIGION

The idea of possibilities is further articulated in Kierkegaard's remarks on Abraham. Abraham had neither surrendered Isaac nor willfully retained him. His faith sustained an 'absurd' certainty that all would be well even though Isaac had been required of him.[37] This unrestrictive attitude toward what might seem to be mutually exclusive possibilities might well be cited as an example of the 'waxing as a whole' of the world of the happy man.

It is essential to notice that the difference in these happy men is not a purely inward qualification. It is not expressed propositionally; one may still look like a tax-collector. But there are consequences for the individual's relations with the world. The perspective of faith is a locus of action and not merely of vision.

The idea of a shift in perspective is clearly evident in the *Tractatus* material about 'the vanishing of the problem' and 'seeing the world aright.'[38] A new understanding, compatible with the idea of 'language-games,' is ushered in by the 1930 assertion that 'language is not a cage.' The possible uses of language are extended substantially. Wittgenstein also continues to reject the idea of a meta-system which can account for these shifts in perspective. But consistent language-use with its own rules is allowed for on both sides of the gap.

Once again this partial understanding could be seen as complete. But once again the problem of fideism arises, joined this time by the problem of relativism. If it is only a question of various self-contained 'games,' then again faith must shun reason. What remains to be shown is that the 'games' are open to interaction.

One of the secular phenomena which Wittgenstein consistently uses to show the presence of various forms of life even within the standard western society is the coronation. Such a ceremony does not have a purpose in the sense of financial transactions or scientific experiments. Nevertheless it has its own rules and its own importance within the everyday world. It is not 'wrong.'[39] This might be a simile for religious actions.

Confusion may arise because the forms of religious language – the surface grammar – may seem to be like that of some other kind of language. (A coronation is built around the everyday action of putting on a hat. Many neighbors of the early Christians had *prima facie* adequate reasons to suppose they practiced cannibalism.) But the deeper grammar of religion has a different slant. For instance, Christianity offers us a (historical) narrative and says: now believe! But not, believe this narrative with the belief appropriate to a historical narrative, rather: believe, through thick and thin, which you can do only as the result of a life. *Here you have a narrative, don't take the same attitude to it as you do to other historical narratives*! Make a *quite different* place in your life for it.[40]

Wittgenstein suggests that the proper attitude to take is 'the attitude that takes a particular matter seriously, but then at a particular point doesn't take it seriously after all, and declares that something else is even more serious.'[41] It is hardly surprising that one might be confused about such a demand.

Kierkegaard's examination of the historical situation of Christian claims is addressed to this confusion. His understanding turns on the idea that the importance of Christian historical claims is quite different from that of ordinary historical claims. It has the ordinary significance and a further dimension. Ordinary historical belief (suspension of skepticism) is required in the case of belief in the historical existence of the man Jesus of Nazareth. (Kierkegaard's insistence on this point is good evidence that he is not a fideist.) But the importance of His existence is not merely that of historical research. Rather, the importance lies in the claim that He is the 'eternal essential Truth.' The evidence on which this is to be believed is far more scant that the evidence of Wittgenstein's interest in religion! The problem is that the claim does look like an ordinary historical claim, albeit an extravagant one: 'The Son of God walked among us as a man.'

Nevertheless there are clues to the proper understanding of the demand to accept this claim, if one is willing to find them. It is a question of examining the surroundings of the expression. 'How words are understood is not told by words alone.'[42] It is only in the context of the application that one can understand the meaning of a word. Wittgenstein provides the clever example of a logarithmic system of measurement, related to the English in that '1 W' = 1 foot – but '2 W' = 4 feet, '3 W' = 9 feet, and so on! Now, do 'This stick is 1 foot long' and 'This stick is 1 W long' really mean the same?[43] Only in the context of the respective systems does either sign make sense; when we try to compare them directly we are at a loss.

Wittgenstein declares himself to be at a loss in this sense when he is confronted with truth-questions about the religious worldview. He remarks that he understands all of the *words* used in describing the Judgement Day. But he is still not in a position to affirm or contradict assertions concerning its occurrence. And when he is asked about the relation between believers and non-believers, he replies: 'My normal technique of language leaves me. I don't know whether to say they understand one another or not.'[44]

A first step out of this dilemma is to realize that an attempt to categorize poetic (or religious) language in factual terms is doomed to failure. We must not forget that 'a poem, even though it is composed in the language of information, is not used in the language-game of giving information.'[45] What is interesting is that we are tempted to forget this. It might be easier to come to terms with something factually very different. No one would be surprised if some extra-terrestrial beings had a form of life very different from ours. What is astonishing is that human beings may be so different that one may hold a scientific worldview and another a religious one. 'Concepts other than though akin to ours might seem *very* queer to us; deviations from the usual *in an unusual direction.*'[46] And indeed they do seem queer. As Wittgenstein points out, concepts basic to scientific studies and those used in religion cut across each other at an angle. Scientific beliefs should be 'well-established.' But the religious believer treats his beliefs as 'well-established' in a way, but again distinctly not so.[47]

Wittgenstein's conception of religion survives the change in his concept of language and philosophy. The language in which it is talked of changes, however. In the 'Lecture on Ethics' he discusses the possibility that scientific investigation could debunk miracles. He suggests that this is impossible. In science there can only be facts, some of which have not yet been subsumed under the scientific system. So 'it is absurd to say "Science has proved that there are no miracles." The truth is that the scientific way of looking at a fact is not the way to look at it as a miracle.'[48] Wittgenstein would certainly not have disagreed with this statement in his later period.

The difference is that in the later philosophy, this other way of looking is not 'beyond language' – although there is something resistant to language about the transition between ways of looking. The experience of the world as a mystical whole is not good scientific evidence. Miracles are not believed on scientific evidence.

IMPLICATIONS FOR RELIGION

But this belief is not a 'blunder.'[49] It is too far different from science, while seeming strangely the same. Religious concepts are 'deviations from the usual *in an unusual direction.*' They seem akin to ordinary ways of speaking in form; but they run in different directions. Wittgenstein cites the difference between 'possibly there is a plane overhead' (which is fairly near to 'there is a plane') and 'possibly there is a Last Judgement' (which is very far from the belief-stance 'there is a Last Judgement').[50] The 'grammar' of this statement is tied up with the very different ways of verifying and using it.

The separation of religion from the categories of science suggests that the essence of religion is not some system. In fact, Wittgenstein himself separates the categories of system and religion repeatedly in the fragments collected as *Culture and Value*. In one set of remarks he talks about doctrine and passion.

> I believe that one of the things Christianity says is that sound doctrines are all useless. That you have to change your *life*. (Or the *direction* of your life.)
>
> It says that wisdom is all cold; and that you can no more use it for setting your life to rights than you can forge iron when it is *cold*.
>
> The point is that a sound doctrine need not *take hold* of you; you can follow it as you would a doctor's prescription. – But here you need something to move you and turn you in a new direction. – (i.e. this is how I understand it.) Once you have been turned round, you must *stay* turned round.
>
> Wisdom is passionless. But faith by contrast is what Kierkegaard calls a *passion*.[51]

Kierkegaard and Wittgenstein both see an interesting isomorphism or family resemblance between the passion required for faith and the inspiration required to 'go on' even in science. For at one level, even a historical assertion is not 'well-founded.' And a doctrine cannot be grasped without some extra-doctrinal understanding and commitment: 'Now I can go on!' One can follow a doctor's prescription, or a timetable; but the method of following is not completely specified by the written matter. In these cases, neither Kierkegaard nor Wittgenstein would be inclined to claim that the

IMPLICATIONS FOR RELIGION

commitment is a conscious one. Kierkegaard calls faith the 'organ of the historical'; it is an inevitable part of that kind of apprehension. Wittgenstein claims that the very idea of doubting some foundation 'facts' is merely a grammatical misunderstanding.

It seems that the case of religion requires another level of grasping. In that case, going through the motions is not enough; being able to go on is not sufficient. Many basic forms of life 'stand fast,' as Wittgenstein says; but there is something slippery about religion. Kierkegaard asserts that the 'stumbling block' of religion is quite intentional. He claims that religious belief must be *'held fast.'*

Part of the added dimension is expressed by Wittgenstein in his remark that religious instruction ought to include an 'appeal to conscience.'[52] This would surely be a stronger appeal than the appeal to reasonable consistency of the person giving instruction in the application of a mathematical formula.

It is hard to make this suggestion square with Wittgenstein's own methods of instruction. Rather (since his objectives in instruction were not wholly religious or ethical), it is hard to see how under his categories an 'appeal to conscience' could have any tangible form. A certain understanding (view) of the facts might grab one's conscience; but understanding in this sense cannot be imparted. Kierkegaard explicitly suggests that such an appeal would be doomed to failure for practical reasons, because it would be viewed as obnoxious by the person appealed to. Still, the idea of such an appeal 'points to something.' Perhaps it might be just an urging to accept the picture presented at a level deeper than that of abstract thought.[53] This level might be manifest as 'always appealing to the picture' or 'always thinking of it.'[54]

Kierkegaard's idea of 'reduplication' has a similar import. 'To reduplicate is to be what one says.'[55] There is a certain kind of reduplication involved in the learning of some mechanical competence; but true reduplication is a phenomenon of the ethical and religious.[56] While competence in mathematics, for example, relates both to logic and to subjective appropriation, 'Christianity is related neither to thinking nor to doubt, but to will and to *obedience*; you shall believe. Wanting to take thinking along is disobedience, no matter whether it says yes or no.'[57]

One certainly could classify religion as a 'form of life' or 'language-game,' in a quasi-metaphysical understanding of these

IMPLICATIONS FOR RELIGION

terms, although this would lead inevitably to accusations of 'relativism.' The idea of 'stages' suggests such a conceptualization. But these last passages suggest that religion considers itself to be at another level. Christian religion in Kierkegaard's understanding claims to be unique, the only right way of looking at the world. But Wittgenstein's scheme of language-games militates against the possibility of one worldview with a privileged position. This appears to be a serious difference between the two authors. But there are clues to a rapprochement.

In this context it is worth remembering that the 'stages' do not constitute a metaphysical scheme. They are not completely separate. Rather, they are linked by the continuity of the individual who passes along 'life's way.' This phrase suggests a linear metaphor, and the inevitable separation of the points along the line. *Either/Or*'s Judge William proposes a better metaphor, that of successive layers. He claims that the aesthetic remains within the ethical, transformed by a superadded 'concentric' shell.[58] And for the Knight of Faith, aesthetic and ethical categories reappear, transformed, in paradoxical religion.

Wittgenstein's 'forms of life' and 'language-games' are also non-metaphysical. The scope of their application is left deliberately vague. Fergus Kerr argues that this scope is bounded, and that nothing as complex and articulated as a religion is the subject of this kind of analysis. It tends to turn on small distinctions.[59] But of course the fundamental differences between the Christian and the non-Christian are not so large regarded factually, the principal dispute being a question of heredity. Surely this is no more complex a difference than a different color-system (which is the example Kerr uses), and surely in both cases the consequences of the difference for everyday life are potentially enormous!

The *Tractatus* analysis of the 'ethical' and 'mystical' suggests the possibility of paradoxical religion outside the categories of human grasping, and hence of a unique kind. The 'absolutely hopeless' running against the walls of our cage is explicitly linked to Kierkegaard's category of 'paradox' by Wittgenstein. He does not focus on the frustration, but on the repeated thrust against the limits, which, he says, points to something.[60]

The situation is apparently changed when Wittgenstein rejects the metaphor of the cage. The idea that religion might be a 'form

IMPLICATIONS FOR RELIGION

of life' is sufficient to give the 'thrust' of religion a place of its own in which to be self-consistent; it no longer must suffer as a misshapen appendage of logically pure language. So 'paradox' is no longer necessary; and apparently religion is no longer unique.

This is perhaps a good place to invoke the idea, mentioned in chapter 2, that the later Wittgenstein is not always the best interpreter of his early writings. The idea of 'paradox' need not reflect the permanent and absolute relations between two language-games or forms of life. Indeed, Kierkegaard's use of the term is not in this vein. Rather, for him it is a transitional category which arises from the inadequacy of the old language-game to the task at hand, and goads the individual into a closer examination of the new language-game. Kierkegaard's explication of the position of the 'spontaneous believer' gives a good statement of his understanding of the dialectics of this situation. What the spontaneous believer (in 'Religiousness A') cannot understand is that what is for him obvious and certain is for others the paradox. But Kierkegaard allows that for the integrated, reduplicated believer (the true Christian, believing the absurd by virtue of the absurd) this dialectical situation is obvious in all its tension – and nevertheless livable.[61]

Wittgenstein's thoughts in this area center on the different ways of 'proving' involved in science and religion. 'Proof' in science has a lot in common with Kierkegaard's 'little Cartesian dolls': the form of the proof is rationally completed, but in order for it to come into force, one must have done with proving, 'let go' of the proof.[62] In science, Wittgenstein allows, there are proofs, but the individual to whom the proof is addressed must eventually see the proof as complete. Explanations end somewhere.

Already in this scheme of proof there is a hint of tension. If it is a matter of 'seeing the proof as complete,' 'coming to an understanding,' there always remains the possibility that one may lose the new understanding. As long as one has the experience 'Now I see!' this tension continues. But understanding changes rapidly from an activity to an ability, from happening to latency. Then the tension is removed, and sometimes great force is needed to renew it.

'Proof' of God's existence does not proceed the same way – or if it does, it is doomed to failure as a convincer. Wittgenstein remarks that a proof of God's existence ought to be sufficient to convince one that God exists. That is what the surface grammar of the expression suggests. The model here would be geometrical proof: 'I will prove to you that there is no such thing as the trisection of an angle with ruler and compass.' But he suggests that reasoned proofs of God's existence are merely attempts by believers to 'give their "belief" an intellectual analysis and foundation, although they themselves would never have come to believe as a result of such proofs.'[63]

The reason for this is that the desire for 'proof of God's existence' is not a request for a causal explanation; instead, it is a demand for the justification of an attitude. Both the search for the answer and the result of finding the answer are only expressible in terms of an individual's life. So the answer must be something having to do with the form of a life. As Kierkegaard remarks, God becomes a necessary postulate, but not in the usual sense; rather, 'the individual's postulation of God is a necessity.'[64]

Kierkegaard is also concerned to show that intellectual proofs are existentially inadequate. His crusade against nominal Christianity stresses the idea of appropriation.

His exposition of this idea proceeds in two directions. One of these trades on the point that even 'purely objective' understandings must have some subjective content, 'for not only is he mad who says what is meaningless, but quite as certainly, he who expresses a correct opinion, when this has absolutely no significance for him.'[65] Two parallel examples might illustrate this point: Kierkegaard's madman, who feigns sanity by incessantly repeating 'Bang, the earth is round';[66] and Wittgenstein's talking lion, whose utterances we could not understand.[67] Only in the flow of a connected form of life, which can only be an individual life (that of an individual in his subjectivity), can objective expressions have meaning.

The second direction in which Kierkegaard's exposition proceeds is from the side of personal need. Christianity's basic claim is of an extreme improbability. Why should anyone believe it? The reason which Kierkegaard supplies is that the potential existential importance of this claim is immense. In effect, if it is 'true' it eliminates (not solves) the 'riddle of life.' It abrogates the problem of finitude, which is the highest and final problem for any contingently existing being.[68] This problem is so important that one has no choice but to grab at the solution.

Wittgenstein suggests that a wholly different kind of instruction is operating in coming to a belief in God. The kind of understanding which this instruction promotes is a wholly different kind of understanding from the seeing of any single thing.

> Life can educate one to a belief in God. And *experiences* too are what bring this about; but I don't mean visions and other forms of sense experience which show us the 'existence of this being,' but, e.g., sufferings of various sorts. These neither show us God in the way a sense impression shows us an object. Nor do they give rise to *conjectures* about him. Experiences, thoughts, – life can force this concept on us.
> So perhaps it is similar to the concept of 'object.'[69]

The suggestion of the last sentence is very helpful. For Wittgenstein the concept of 'object' is a complex one. It is certainly useful, but it cannot be reduced to any metaphysical or observational definition.[70] It is almost paradigmatic of the foundational, but nonetheless 'not-well-founded' concept.

This association is consistent with his remarks about the status of religious belief in the lectures on religious belief. There the believer's view is said to show itself 'not by reasoning or by appeal to ordinary grounds for belief, but rather by regulating for in all his life [*sic*].'[71] Christianity rightly understood is a 'firmly rooted [not *proven*] picture,' and in this sense has more to do grammatically with superstition than with scientific fact. For this reason, all philosophy written about it (under the assumption that it is founded at a higher level of gaming) is doomed to reach false conclusions.[72]

Kierkegaard goes further along the same line, claiming that religious life is radically grounded. So it could hardly be an occasion for giving grounds. The religiously aware self 'rests [is grounded] transparently in the Power that established it.'[73]

Citing the grammatical similarity of religion and superstition as against the grammar of fact is not of course to suggest that they are similar in application. Wittgenstein remarks an obvious difference: superstition is a sort of 'false science' (an untrue causal nexus) whereas religion depends on trust and at important junctures rejects the causal nexus.[74] In this dimension superstition is more similar to science than it is to religion. But that only goes to show that the three ways of thinking cannot be subsumed under a system.

IMPLICATIONS FOR RELIGION

One way in which religion might claim to be unique is that it lacks much of the superstructure of ordinary language-games. Or rather, the superstructure exists, but it is not essential to the continuation of the category. Science has not only a way of looking at the world, but empirical methods and data derived from this basic belief-structure. One cannot 'do science' without both the way of looking and the experimental method. The religious or 'ethical' way of looking at the world provides a basic way of understanding things, but leaves the actual activities (to be informed by this way of looking) unspecified. A scientist is always called a scientist, but only 'does science' when he is actually experimenting, lecturing, and so forth. A religious believer is *always* a religious believer, and cannot choose to continue or stop 'doing religion.'

In other words, the tension involved in the transition to religion does not go away. The religious seeker or believer remains at the stage of activity, and does not attain comfortable latency.

Kierkegaard's categories of 'mystery' and 'paradox' turn on this continuation of activity. The religious believer is living in two worlds at once. She has regard to two grammars, the everyday grammar of the world and the grammar of religious faith. These two grammars are not fully separate, but 'cut each other at an angle.' Either might 'stand fast' in latency; but to keep the two in tension requires the believer to 'hold fast.' Such an existence in tension, with an 'absolute relation to the absolute *telos* and a relative relation to relative ends,' is paradoxical.

Wittgenstein's understanding of the connection of ethics, life, and philosophical investigations is an example of a similar tension. Unlike Hume, who could put away his reflections on the ill-foundedness of causal connection in order to go to dinner, Wittgenstein could not put away his philosophy. It informed his everyday life, and he disliked intensely the type of philosophers whose philosophy did not do so. The idea that philosophy and religious life are *activities* (and not bodies of doctrine) leads to this entanglement with 'conscience.'

This suggests another facet to the phenomenon of religion: the religious belief-scheme can be added on to other schemes. There are, for example, religious physical scientists. There could hardly be superstitious physical scientists.

Because of its unique status, religion cannot be completely

separated from the ordinary world. For instance, the explanatory language of religion owes a lot to the language of ordinary life.

> Could you explain the concept of the punishments of hell without using the concept of punishment? Or that of God's goodness without using the concept of goodness?
> If you want to get the right *effect* with your words, certainly not.[75]

Anyone who has received a certain sort of education can understand what is going on in religious truth-claims, in a sense. Of course, the language of religious convincing, which is aimed at the non-believer, must be pitched in terms which the non-believer can understand. Otherwise, the 'effect' will be lost. But this is merely another expression of the tension between the believer and the world.[76]

Wittgenstein's 'ethical' concern can be explicated in terms of the special status of religion. His concern would not be to eliminate science or even philosophy. Rather it would be to make the 'mystical' understanding part of the perspective. Since this understanding is at the most basic level (as fundamental as the concept 'object,' if not more so) it need not conflict with any factual information. Given the opportunity to 'see the world aright,' an individual may come to a better understanding of all facts.

This presents an added reason why the idea of any religion as a 'system' must be rejected. The very idea of 'system' is a category of scientific thought. To present 'system' or 'understanding' as an absolute is to make a category-mistake.

There is of course a way in which the 'mystical' way of living is demonically aped. This is the 'scientific' trap of the 'loss of deep problems.' Where the 'mystical' rests on a sublime confidence in the dissolution of all such problems, this false consciousness has a ridiculous confidence in their non-existence. It is interesting to note that Wittgenstein quotes in this connection a saying from Augustine: 'quia plus loquitur inquisitio quam inventio,'[77] which parallels one of Kierkegaard's favorite mottoes, 'attributable to Lessing:' 'If God held all truth in His right hand, and in His left the lifelong pursuit of it, he [Lessing] would choose the left hand.'[78] This accentuates that the essence of religion lies in the form of the religious life, and not in the factual content nor in the 'results' (scientifically understood) of that life.

IMPLICATIONS FOR RELIGION

Even in the context of Wittgenstein's later understanding of the relation of language-games, then, there is at least one feature of religion that remains unique, or at least highly unusual. This is the religious individual's intentional maintenance in the tension of multiple language-games – because she participates in one particular game, the religious, which looks over the shoulder of all others. The tension inherent in the religious position is magnified in that the game itself demands a paradoxical openness to change.

If there is another language-game that makes similar demands, it is philosophy. The philosopher also applies the toolbox which constitutes her specialty in an examination of other games. Wittgenstein's persistent understanding of the connection between philosophy and lived ethics finds itself justified by this point. But philosophy and religion diverge in one essential way: the key to philosophy is ability to stop doing it;[79] whereas the key to religion is inability to stop doing it. When the metaphysical framework of worldviews first suggested by the idea of the 'stages' or 'language-games' is rejected, and this multiplicity of levels of grasping substituted, then there is no problem admitting the usefulness (and at the same time inadequacy) of reason for religion. The problem of fideism will not be solved, but dissolved.

In the course of unravelling Wittgenstein's position on the question of religion (and enlightening Kierkegaard's), we have uncovered two ironies. First of all, Wittgenstein's earlier and later positions seem remarkably unified on this question. Certainly Wittgenstein always understood there to be an essential connection between his earlier and later work. He wanted to have the *Tractatus* and the *Investigations* published together. Nor could this be entirely because the later work served as a mere appendix of corrections to the earlier. It points out fundamental errors in some underlying assumptions, but what Wittgenstein called the 'point of the book' (the material on the ethical and the mystical) goes unchallenged. In fact, the framework of the later understanding is more felicitous to the ethical points! To use Kierkegaard's terminology, it has become clear that Wittgenstein is not a 'premise-author.'

The second irony uncovered is that Kierkegaard, 'a religious writer,' and Wittgenstein, 'not a religious writer,' are close enough on key points that (at the very least) examples from each lend support to the understanding of the other. There is now no way of

IMPLICATIONS FOR RELIGION

knowing how much of the material on religion collected in *Culture and Value*, which has a distinctly 'Kierkegaardian' ring, was directly influenced by Wittgenstein's reading of Kierkegaard. Certainly it is not merely parroted, but is further developed. What is more interesting is that the whole scheme of Wittgenstein's later works lends itself to congruity with a Kierkegaardian analysis of religion.

This compatibility of Wittgenstein's work with religion ought to have been foreseen. Even though he did not feel a religious vocation in any conventional sense, nevertheless his own personal feeling of need in this direction informed his philosophical work. It might even be suggested that his stress on the individual appropriation of facts is based on an ethical pattern. Ethical decisions cannot be forced on the individual; they must be freely made. His understanding of the importance of the ethical led inevitably to a philosophical conception in which such free acceptance is not only possible but necessary.[80]

The conception of religion suggested above has important consequences for possible positions on some of the most important arguments in philosophy of religion. One such argument is theodicy.

Theodicies tend to depend either on metaphysical points or on epistemologies. That is, either evil is justified as metaphysically inevitable, or it is denied as a false perception following from limited human understanding. (Many theodicies have strands of both types.) Classically, at least in the West, factual (propositional) arguments are used and general solutions are proposed.

The understanding promulgated by Kierkegaard and Wittgenstein demands a shifting of the ground of the argument. In keeping with their way of working, conceptual revisions might be suggested and the dimension of personal acceptance stressed. Wittgenstein's 'world of the happy man' and Kierkegaard's 'perspective of faith' are both implicit theodicies. They constitute dissolutions (vanishings) of the problem of evil.[81] At the same time, the tension implicit in the religious person's participation in the world ensures that the problem remains essential.

The appeal to the individual is a particularly important factor here. Many theodicies fail to take it into account, with the result that they cannot as effectively address the very personal nature of evil as a life-experience.[82] Wittgenstein's remark that 'proofs' of God are not the reasons or causes for their authors' belief in God stands as a pointer in the direction of more existential theodicy.

Finally it is worth noting that Wittgenstein's position on religion has consequences for his 'relativism.' It has been said that relativism is a position at which Wittgenstein arrives quite consciously, and not one which he falls into or begins from unconsciously.[83] His stress on the ethical – his form of religion – suggests a modification of the idea that he is a relativist. The ethical as a superadded form of life would provide grounds for the selection of language-games. As such it would act to limit relativism. This is not to say that everyone will share in this form of life. But here Wittgenstein is 'leaving everything as it is.' Relativists do exist. And relativism is surely not a mistake about facts, but a question of interpretation. So relativists must be *shown* the path to ethics. Wittgenstein might well subscribe to Kierkegaard's claim that the existential value of holding the 'ethical' or religious worldview is a substantial inducement to accept it.

Granted that this is not a form of metaphysical absolutism. But the form of relativism it is intended to combat is not metaphysical either. It is an absolutism of values aimed at making sense of the maze of existential possibilities and problems. What drives it is the absolute value of the individual's life. The standard which the 'ethical' upholds is the value *for* the individual's life.[84] The postulation of this existential either/or is the closest that either Kierkegaard or Wittgenstein will come to admitting a metaphysical certainty for existing beings.

Chapter Five

ECHOES AND REPERCUSSIONS

In prior chapters, attention has been focused on some problems with which Kierkegaard and Wittgenstein deal explicitly, or with questions arising from their method of dealing with these problems. But at the end of chapter 4, the possibility of a theodicy implicit in the work of the two authors was suggested. This possibility raises the specter of larger questions: What features of the work of Kierkegaard and Wittgenstein give their conclusions a more general interest? What lasting impact might their considerations have on the practice of 'philosophizing'?

One essential part of an answer to these questions is an understanding of what would count as 'continuing to do philosophy in the vein of Kierkegaard and Wittgenstein.'

If either thinker propounded straightforward theories, such an understanding would be easier to gain. For instance, triadic structures, universal histories, and systematic phenomenologies of spirit mark the 'young Hegelians' as disciples of Hegel. Stylistic innovations are relatively unimportant. With Kierkegaard and Wittgenstein, however, it is precisely the innovations of style and method which must be considered.

Some similarities between the two authors' work are mentioned in chapter 2. But it can hardly be a case of demanding exactly similar methods in the consideration of other questions. Both Kierkegaard and Wittgenstein are so idiosyncratic – in fact their own methodologies are so internally diverse – that it can only be a matter of searching for, or attempting to adhere to, certain 'family resemblances' in the working out of various problems. To demand more than this would have the ironic consequence of – as Kierkegaard puts it – turning their indirection into a 'result.'[1]

A better criterion for the consideration of extensions might be the sense of a new spirit in which both Wittgenstein and Kierkegaard share. Their methodological innovations are often bound up with this sense of new spirit. Provided that remarks are offered in the appropriate spirit, their substance might be given relatively little weight. But a question then arises as to how a work is to be recognized as 'in the spirit,' if not by any theoretical content or specific methodology followed.

A final criterion to be kept in mind, and one which may be able to mitigate the problems implied by the previous two, is that of personal involvement. Both authors were distinguished by their involvement with their work, as well as their demands that their readers should be similarly involved. Thus some personal dimension may be the ultimate mark of adherence to this new philosophical form.

Of course, one important source to be considered in any attempt to suggest that the two authors' work has relevance for further and larger questions is a review of their own ideas concerning the possibility of such extensions. Both displayed a well-founded pessimism concerning the likelihood, if not the feasibility, of worthwhile continuations.

In the context of the current task, Kierkegaard's remarks on his own way of working, and on the way in which Christianity can be communicated, are particularly relevant. The following comment from the *Postscript* illustrates his conception of the difference between the methods of the systematic philosophers and those of the Christian tradition.

> In relation to a doctrine, understanding is the maximum of what may be attained; to become an adherent is merely an artful method of pretending to understand, practiced by people who do not understand anything. In relation to an existential communication, existing in it is the maximum of attainment, and understanding it is merely an evasion of the task. It is a suspicious thing to become a Hegelian, understanding Hegel is the maximum; to become a Christian is the maximum, Christianity is suspect. . . . To seek to understand an existential communication is to essay a transformation of one's own relationship to it into one of possibility merely.[2]

Kierkegaard so stresses the category of 'appropriation,' both in everyday matters and in the more essential pursuit of religion, that it would be strange to abandon it in attempting to extend his vision. Thus a first approximation at the road to be taken by sincere followers of Kierkegaard might well read: 'Understanding Kierkegaard is absolutely odd; to be a Kierkegaardian is the ideal.'

This suggestion needs to be understood in the right sense, however. In *The Concept of Anxiety*, Vigilius Haufniensis remarks: 'There is an old saying that to understand and to understand are two things, and so they are.'[3] In the same vein, to appropriate and to appropriate may be quite different things. To borrow (appropriate) the idea of appropriation, to speak systematically of it, and to attempt to formalize the possibilities inherent in the category, would not be in the spirit of 'existence-communication.' Kierkegaard tells the story of the drill sergeant and the recruit who is talking in the ranks. The sergeant yells 'Shut up!'; the recruit answers back: 'Yes, of course, now that I know you want me to, I'll shut up!' This is a prime example of an existence-communication being misunderstood as an academic lecture.[4]

Kierkegaard stresses the appropriate attitude to existence-communication in his comments on edification. In *Purity of Heart*, he defines the listener's role in a devotional address. The listener is to take the address personally. The speaker is to do the same. In one sense the speaker is a mere 'prompter,' giving each listener pause and reflection; but he is himself also a responsible individual – responsible for what he is saying.[5] Speaker and listeners reflectively appropriate the content of the address.

The example of the devotional address is useful as an illustration of Kierkegaard's idea of 'reduplication.' To reduplicate oneself is to 'be what one says.'[6] Dialectical truth is 'raised to the second power' in lived action. It is a question of *how* as well as *what*.[7]

While Kierkegaard's analysis applies specifically to the religious sphere (although, thanks to his specific 'problem,' in so doing it deals with human existence in general), Wittgenstein had similar ideas in relation to the way in which philosophy ought to be done. He once remarked that if a philosophy book was any good, it should frustrate the reader so much that he would want to throw it across the room and start on the problems fresh for himself, thus 'reduplicating' the author's work.[8] A great work might even cause lived reduplication; it might cause a change in the reader's life based on the results of his deliberations. In several forewords and prefaces, Wittgenstein expressed the hope – though not the expectation – that his works might have this effect.

Wittgenstein displays an ambivalence toward the whole idea of having his work continued. He could never found a school, he says, because he is 'by no means sure that [he] should prefer a continuation of [his] work by others to a change in the way people live which would make all of these questions superfluous.'[9] He also remarks that he does not want to be imitated, at any rate not by philosophical writers. And he harbors a fundamental pessimism concerning the idea of important change caused by philosophical writing: it may be, he remarks, that the impetus for the kind of change philosophers want must come from another direction entirely. Only the most indirect influence has a fair chance of success.[10]

This ambivalence accords well with his belief that philosophy is not an end in itself, but something that, if properly handled, clears up muddles then shuts itself off. But the more interesting implication of these comments is the pointer toward what *is* important, or an end in itself, if philosophy is not. Philosophy is in the service of a larger goal: fundamental change in peoples' lives. Here there is once again a reduplicated notion: philosophy is a task, but merely a sub-task of the larger task. Life itself is the larger task. (Recall Engelmann's statement: 'He saw life as a task.') If philosophy is not an end in itself, there is no reason why its methods should be anything other than *ad hoc*.

Commentaries on Wittgenstein's remarks about the way to do philosophy have been afflicted by precisely the sort of misunderstanding satirized by Kierkegaard in the story of the recruit and the drill sergeant. Wittgenstein once remarked that he was afraid that the only result of his teaching was to sow the seeds of a jargon; at least one interpreter has reluctantly agreed with that gloomy assessment. Wittgenstein's idea of eliminating muddles in philosophy has been given lip service, but not necessarily applied. Somehow 'Wittgensteinian' philosophy seems a particularly good example of the complaint expressed by A in *Either/Or*: the sign in the philosophical shop window reads PRESSING DONE HERE; but if you unpacked your philosophical baggage on the counter in the expectation of having the muddles expertly removed, you would be disappointed – it is the *claim* to remove muddles which is being retailed, and not the actual removing![11]

This parable suggests another pitfall on the opposite side from the error of dogmatism which Kierkegaard so ably deciphers in Hegel. Rather, it is the same error, but in another guise: the failure to appropriate. Hegel espoused system at the expense of existence and appropriation; to espouse appropriation, but at the expense of existential appropriation, would be an ironically potentiated error.

Kierkegaard's understanding of his 'task' concerning Christianity provides an exact parallel of, if not a model for, Wittgenstein's notion of philosophy. He uses a variety of tools in carrying out the task. Some of his writings are aesthetic, and others philosophical, in expression. An underlying form is provided by his psychological analysis. This analysis suggests a rationale for the form of the various writings. But even the psychological framework is in the service of the 'task'; it is not an end in itself. Thus there is no motivation for the technique to be maintained when another might be of greater usefulness. The new methodology of the 'attack,' in the *Fatherland* and the *Moment*, may be freely adopted.

Kierkegaard tended to set himself up as absolutely different from other theologians and philosophers. But Wittgenstein did give some account of a difference (which presupposes a connection) between his way of philosophizing and traditional philosophy. This account might serve as the basis for continued philosophical work in a 'Wittgensteinian' vein. G. E. Moore's report on lectures and discussions held by Wittgenstein in the academic years 1930-1 and 1932-3 contains a brief section reporting Wittgenstein's comments on this point.[12]

In the lectures, Wittgenstein remarked that he thought there had been 'kink' in the development of philosophy (presumably in or as a result of his work), similar to the development of chemistry from alchemy. This kink had made it possible that there should be *skillful* philosophers, whereas previously advances had only been made by 'great' ones.

Wittgenstein did not elaborate on this point, and his exact meaning is not immediately clear. The difference between alchemy and chemistry lies in the kind of questions asked, and the kind of answers expected. Chemistry's approach is experimental and incremental, depending less on great leaps and more on answers to particular questions. There is also a fundamental change in the understanding of causality underlying these questions and answers.

The difference between the *Tractatus* understanding of philosophy (which is expressed as an extension of the tradition of logical analysis) and the later understanding is also rooted in a change in the understanding of causality, accompanied by a reduction in the scope of individual questions. The *Tractatus* presupposes the 'mental object' and even 'mental process' model. The later works deny this causal nexus.

Some advances in chemistry and medicine were made by alchemists – for example, by Paracelsus. But these were great geniuses. They were able to make advances despite the handicap of a relatively unfruitful model of reality. But the basic laws of chemistry stand like signposts away from the errors of alchemy. Thus it is easy to avoid error, if not to achieve great breakthroughs. Wittgenstein's suggestions about the differentiation of language might stand as similar signposts in philosophy. He may have believed that in their light it would be possible to solve particular problems of an everyday kind with some regularity, if not to make great advances.

The obvious connection between the new way and the old consists in the continuity of basic subject matter, the foundational (and nagging!) nature of the expressed concerns, and the claim to offer a solution of these problems – even if the solution turns out to be something not envisioned in the original search. Here Wittgenstein used the simile of the attempt to trisect an angle with ruler and compass. A proof that this is impossible would satisfy a geometer who had been attempting it, although it would not be the original or envisioned object of his search. Kierkegaard's remarks about reason's collision with the 'thing that thought cannot think' suggest the same kind of unexpected result. If reason is 'seeking its own downfall,' it could hardly hope for a more felicitous downfall than that promised by the Absolute Paradox.[13] Just as the geometer seeks a positive result and is satisfied by a negative demonstration, so reason, in seeking a negation, encounters at the same time the ultimate positive claim.

Of course, while reason's approach to the paradoxical boundary is clear to see, the direction taken by faith in going on from the boundary is not so clear. The same sort of difficulty arises in the attempt to understand how Wittgenstein intended philosophy to 'go on' from the cusp he had created. While it is possible to see what is held in common (the goals) and what is rejected by Wittgenstein (the old method and way of expression), the positive suggestions concerning the new direction to be taken after the 'kink' are more difficult to nail down, perhaps more difficult than he anticipated.

Wittgenstein attached the greatest importance to the methods used. In the 1930–3 lectures, he referred to his philosophizing as being synoptic of trivialities, already known; 'if we leave out any, we still have the feeling that something is wrong.' He thought that this method required a kind of thinking different from the scientific, and requiring discussion to be learned and carried out. Most interestingly, 'As regards his own work, he said it did not matter whether his results were true or not: what mattered was that "a method had been found."'[14] This assertion is astounding when taken in comparison with the *Tractatus* comment that the definitive solution to the problems examined had already been found. Rather than claiming to have completed the task of philosophy, the later Wittgenstein merely claimed to have generated the mechanism by which one would be able to desist when appropriate.

This claim is isomorphic with Kierkegaard's discussion of the kind of continuation which follows the leap of faith. Hegel sought to go further than faith; Kierkegaard preferred the idea of continuation *in* faith. The Knight of Faith does not 'remain standing,' but holds fast in an active sense.[15] Having a particular solution, he does not continue toward a chimerical definitive solution.

The scope of Wittgenstein's claims of achievement is further reduced when the actual working of the method he proposed is recalled. The method is one of problem solving. There is not one single problem ('the riddle of life?') but many difficulties. So there cannot be a single method, but multiple methods: 'like different therapies.'[16]

This feature is clearly shadowed by Kierkegaard's 'authorship.' For him there is of course a single problem; but within this problem there are nevertheless many difficulties. Each stage, and even each individual, must be addressed in a slightly different way. The operators of change from the aesthetic to the ethical are quite different from those provoking the transition to the religious. The philosophically oriented *Fragments* and *Postscript*, the psychologically expressed *Concept of Anxiety* and *Sickness Unto Death*, and the more literary *Either/Or* and *Repetition* each approach the task from a different direction. The openly religious tone of the *Edifying*

Discourses provides yet another supplement to the therapy.

Some clarification of the proposed change in methodology may come from two remarks. One concerns the usefulness of 'masks' in the educational process: 'an educator never says what he himself thinks, but only what he thinks of a subject in relation to the profit of him who he is educating.'[17] But the author of this statement nevertheless claims unity for his authorship, though he despairs of anyone's noticing it: 'That the long logic of a quite determinate philosophical *sensibility* is involved here, and not a confusion of a hundred indiscriminate paradoxes and heterodoxies; of that, I believe, nothing has dawned even on my most benevolent readers.'[18] These comments made by Nietzsche quite fairly represent the schema of the new methodology attempted by Kierkegaard and Wittgenstein. It ought to be remembered, though, that for our two authors the audience of the educator always includes the educator himself. So perhaps it would be more appropriate to speak of metamorphoses, rather than masks. But this methodology clearly requires that the audience miss the speaker's larger intentions, since the hearers must be brought to the point at which they can go on. The speaker can expect little glory. It is interesting to note that Kierkegaard and Wittgenstein (and Nietzsche, as the above material illustrates) were all annoyed and saddened by the failure of their audiences to give them due credit, even though this failure was accounted for and expected according to their own explicit ideas.

Kierkegaard's and Wittgenstein's concern with methodology is an expression of the fundamental difference in their conception of philosophy. The idea of philosophy against which they are reacting is that of the search for foundations and the construction of a unified understanding of the world. Metaphysical concerns are central to such a philosophical system.

The philosopher's use of multiple methods, masks, and metamorphoses is the last step in the breakdown of monolithic 'Philosophy' which begins with the transition from factual investigation to conceptual investigation. As is usual with both Kierkegaard and Wittgenstein, this transition has consequences at many levels. One of these is the new understanding of previously recognized similarities and definitions in terms of 'family resemblance.' Another is the recognition of many 'forms of life' and 'language-games.' While the challenge of metaphysics is to unify the world in understanding, the new challenge is to conceive a set of tools which are capable of generating some useful results in many of the parts of the fractured existing world.

Strategies of communication and the connections within existential experience help to cross the boundaries of forms of life in the new style of philosophy. For instance, Wittgenstein's extended notion of the concept 'grammar' serves (among other things) as a convenient hook or common conceptual feature of the various fragments. This concept serves both to connect forms of life (to show their family resemblance) and to separate them. It is a point of application for philosophical therapies. In many cases, Wittgensteinian philosophical arguments take their root in a comparison of the actual 'grammar' of deeds (existential happenings, linguistic or otherwise) and the understanding of these deeds reflected in language. For instance, the surface grammar of 'mental process' words like 'to know' and 'to think' is similar to that of 'to have' and 'to do.' In the *Investigations*, the actual features of 'knowing,' 'expecting someone,' 'calling someone to mind,' and other phenomena of experience are recalled. It becomes clear that these expressions actually function in a wide variety of ways, mostly quite different from the ways in which terms denoting external actions do.

Many of Kierkegaard's works use the same strategy of revealing another grammar under the surface. The analysis of life as 'despair' in *The Sickness Unto Death* and the revelation of the aesthete's pose in *Either/Or* are good examples. The demonstration that many forms of life are nevertheless guises for despair, the 'sickness unto death' which can never actually result in death, shares many features with Wittgenstein's analysis of philosophy as a 'sickness,' which despite its constant drive for explanations of the world never achieves its goal.[19]

One important feature of Wittgenstein's conceptual investigations is the recognition of vast differences between language-games in the meanings of basic words common to many games. The motto which he had imagined taking, 'I'll teach you differences,' comes to mind.[20] It is worth noting that Kierkegaard's work tacitly uses the same recognition. For instance, in *Either/Or* the title term has distinct meanings for the aesthete (who uses the term ironically), the ethicist (who demands lawful choice), and the religious figure of the 'Ultimatum' (who negates the ethical choice, which can only be returned in faith through grace). A recognition of this differentiation in usage is intended to shock the reader into a reconsideration of his own use of the term.

Kierkegaard pursues this idea in several of the edifying works. In *Judge for Yourselves* he notes that Christ is far more terrible than any worldly robber or slanderer. For the one who takes my money or my reputation is nevertheless agreed that money and reputation are worthwhile. But Christ, by his life, denied the value of goods and reputation. He has 'taken' these things from us far more surely and decisively than any human enemy could.[21]

The discourse on the topic 'The righteous man strives in prayer with God and conquers – in that God conquers' expresses a similar revision of the idea of worth in connection with prayer. A Christian might describe prayer as 'profitable'; but it would scarcely benefit a sensualist to hear it so described, since there would be no agreement between them on the meaning of the word.[22] The 'result' of prayer seems intensely ironic in the worldly sense – it is no tangible result (no change) at all. But from the perspective of faith it is a result.

Despite the anti-metaphysical bias of the two authors, there is yet in both an important strategic place for empirical facts. Kierkegaard's empirical psychology is a fine example of this place. (While many of his examples are overdrawn, they are nevertheless closely enough rooted in reality to be able to serve as mirrors for his readers.) His dependence on 'reason' to separate 'nonsense' from the 'absurd' is another way in which he contacts the empirical. So is his demand for Christian consistency: doing as well as saying. Wittgenstein's reliance on examples from the real world is comparable. Both also used made-up stories – things which look like facts, and serve in a role similar to that filled by facts, but which are at the closest only exaggerations of actual situations. Wittgenstein refers to them as 'intermediate examples.'[23]

Because Wittgenstein proposes the idea of various *ad hoc* philosophical 'therapies,' it is hard to think of any well-defined philosophical movement as possibly 'Wittgensteinian.' (It is even harder to imagine what might be 'Kierkegaardian.') In the lectures reported by Moore, Wittgenstein mentioned in passing two points that help to define his attitude toward two of the directions in which his work has actually been developed. He rejects the idea that philosophy is 'analytic.' (He prefers the term 'synoptic.') It is not a question of breaking down some compound, as a chemist might. While the immediate and obvious referent of this comment is Wittgenstein's own earlier work on the analysis of propositions, it might also serve as a suggestion on the method to be followed in philosophy. Individual instances cannot be analyzed; only systems, groups, and multiple examples can build up the picture required.

Wittgenstein also made reference to the philosophical study of language. His own works remark on certain grammatical constructions as fostering misleading pictures. But other (material or visual) analogies may be equally misleading. (For instance, object-metaphysics is surely based on features of the sensible world, and not merely on subject/predicate grammar.) He did not think that language in general was or should be the subject of philosophy.[24] His extended use of the term 'grammar,' and the large role which language in fact plays in many forms of life, may be misleading in this regard. In this context, it is important to remember that he understood language as merely one form of 'the deed.'[25]

It would of course be presumptuous to reject 'analytic' and 'linguistic' philosophy as participants in the true Grail quest – if any! – simply on the basis of these paltry references. They do reflect a general tendency on the part of Wittgenstein to appreciate wider variety in many areas. Not just language, but all kinds of deeds are interesting.[26] Not just one example, but many are to be examined. The 'one-sided diet' was a philosophical danger of which he was well aware.

Kierkegaard certainly shared this tendency. He found grist for his religious mill in areas as far afield as seduction, literary criticism, and a battle against yellow journalism. He also rejected the pat answers of Hegelianism.

Despite (or perhaps on account of) the above-mentioned tendency to breadth, there is a problem in determining just what features one would look for in the search for the true successors to Wittgenstein's and Kierkegaard's work. Kierkegaard's rejection of Hegel seems clear enough; but his rejection of Adler clouds matters again. That is, dogma is clearly rejected, and some sort of methodological recommendation put in its place. But the source of guidelines for following this recommendation is far from clear. The same sort of difficulty led the positivists to believe that Wittgenstein was denying the importance of the unsayable.

This problem is a fine instance of the more general problem of 'going on,' which plays such a large part in the problems both authors investigated. Different understandings of the acts involved can lead to different assessments of the appropriate way of continuing the series. It is more a question of continuing in the same *spirit* than of hewing to any theoretical rules.

Wittgenstein's Foreword to the typescript now published as *Philosophical Remarks* gives some further clues as to a possible working out of the process. He writes:

> This book is written for such men as are in sympathy with its spirit. This spirit is different from the one which informs the vast stream of European and American civilization in which all of us stand. *That* spirit expresses itself in an onwards movement, in building ever larger and more complicated structures; the other in striving after clarity and perspicuity in no matter what structure. The first tries to grasp the world by way of its periphery – in its variety; the second at its centre – in its essence. And so the first adds one construction to another, moving on and up, as it were, from one stage to the next, while the other remains where it is and what it tries to grasp is always the same.
>
> I would like to say 'This book is written to the glory of God,' but nowadays that would be chicanery, that is, it would not be rightly understood. It means the book is written in good will, and in so far as it is not so written, but out of vanity, etc., the author would wish to see it condemned. He cannot free it of these impurities further than he himself is free of them.[27]

There are many dimensions to this statement. One of the most obvious themes is a stress on the divorce between the methods of Wittgensteinian 'philosophy' and those traditionally associated with physical science. But at a deeper level this stress presupposes the possibility of the divorce. The whole project of extending factual understanding – 'grasping the world at its periphery' – which might easily be (has in fact been) understood as a paradigm for all advancement of human ends, is radically relativised.

'Understanding' is relativised in one sense simply by the introduction of the project of grasping at the center, with perspicuity. The mere fact that such a project could be conceived, and an attempt made to carry it through, demonstrates this relativising. As Wittgenstein remarked, what is essential is that a method has been found.

The idea of 'concentricity' mentioned in *Either/Or* is worth recalling in this context. It too suggests a centered mode of development in which forward motion is not essential or even desirable.

The second paragraph of the Foreword suggests another kind of relativising. The author expresses an extremely personal involvement with the work. He does *not* say that he would wish to see condemned the parts of the book which are shown to be inaccurate, factually misleading, or plain wrong. Rather, he places a premium on the 'good will' with which the investigation has been carried out. This shift in emphasis recalls Kierkegaard's claim about the individual's relation to the 'eternal essential truth':

> When the question of the truth is raised subjectively, reflection is directed subjectively to the nature of the individual's relationship; if only the mode of this relationship is in the truth, the individual is in the truth even if he should happen to be thus related to what is not true.[28]

For Kierkegaard this analysis is part of an argument denying the possibility of systematic religious knowledge. For Wittgenstein, the parallel analysis is brought to a more secular problem. It is not the case that Kierkegaard did not believe the problem to occur at the mundane level.[29] But he thought that the 'approximation-process' of rational discovery could provide a sufficient solution to the problem at that level. The higher degree of personal certainty provided by the '*appropriation*-process' ought to be unnecessary, or at least unconscious.

One phenomenon Wittgenstein noticed is that philosophy dredges the question of personal certainty up from the unconscious level. His project – to demonstrate the possibility of being able to stop doing philosophy – seeks the reasons and tools whereby this question can be dismissed again. He tries to show that there are limits to objective inquiry, and that there is nothing inherently *wrong* with the fact that there are limits. He also tries to suggest what happens when traditional philosophy tries to transcend these limits. The discussion of 'going on' is an attempt to fathom the appropriation-process, which takes up where philosophy *must* leave off.

Wittgenstein's careful charting of the difference between his spirit and that of western science mirrors a distinction made by Kierkegaard. The Excelsior spirit of 'moving on and up,' to which Wittgenstein contrasts his interest in constantly reviewing the center, accords well with the Hegelian category 'going further' so disdained by Kierkegaard.

Both Kierkegaard and Wittgenstein recognize that abstaining from 'going further' does not eliminate the necessity to 'go on.' For Kierkegaard this necessity is rooted in the essential difficulty and existential necessity of faith. One cannot 'remain standing' at faith, because being faithful is a full-time job.[30]

Wittgenstein's reasons to 'go on' in philosophy are more secular, if no less existential. New problems are always arising in the course of life. Thus even if one is able to stop doing philosophy when one wants – to call a halt to the infinite regress of metaphysics – there will constantly be new occasion to make philosophical decisions, and constant temptation to return to metaphysical speculation.

The form of Wittgenstein's writings, and the switch in emphasis from 'truth' to 'good faith,' suggest another dimension to the rethinking of intellectual activity. Understanding has come to attain near-teleological status in modern western thought. If 'a little knowledge is a dangerous thing,' the standard reasoning goes, the antidote to this danger must be an increase in the quantity of knowledge. A continuous effort is made to expand the periphery of the world. This undertaking has a life of its own; it is understood as good in itself.

Kierkegaard's criticism of objectivity and Wittgenstein's project of re-grasping the world at its center both oppose themselves to the 'spirit' of this project. Both take a very complex view of factual knowledge.

For Kierkegaard, understanding prevents the assent to nonsense, but it cannot force the assent to essential paradox. Yet without appropriation, the most ordinary statements become ridiculous; a madman can repeat every five seconds 'the earth is round,' and this alone will mark him as mad.

For Wittgenstein, in one sense, the factual is merely prolegomenon. The subjective interpretation of the facts is the essential part. Philosophy 'leaves everything as it is,' but it allows us to see things differently. In another sense, the 'factual' is the end of the process. Only as a result of subjective informing can there be any 'facts' at all. At the least, then, the individual's subjectivity is an equal partner with the facts.

At this point there is again a connection between the work of Kierkegaard and Wittgenstein, and that of Nietzsche. He remarks:

> Against positivism, which halts at phenomena – 'There are only *facts*' – I would say: No, facts is precisely what there is not, only interpretations. . . .
>
> In so far as the word 'knowledge' has any meaning, the world is knowable; but it is *interpretable* otherwise, it has no meaning behind it, but countless meanings – 'Perspectivism.'[31]

In this succinct formulation, Nietzsche distills a large part of the shift in perspective carried out by Kierkegaard and Wittgenstein, which is at the same time a proposal for a revision in the understanding of philosophy and an attempt to be true to this proposal.

It is important to understand that (at least in the case of Kierkegaard and Wittgenstein) this shift in perspective to a recommendation of perspectivism is not a metaphysical demand. Rather, it is a call for a shift in emphasis away from the metaphysical (and the worldview in which it has its origins) in general.

The revision away from facts and toward perspectives suggests the need for a new source of certainty. If knowledge cannot be based on metaphysical foundations, then it must have some other foundation. It is at this point that the dimension Kierkegaard calls 'passion' and Wittgenstein refers to as the 'ethical' comes into play.

A reminder is in order here that the point at which passion becomes necessary is not so far down the path, even for Kierkegaard. In the *Fragments*, he remarks that (limited) faith is already required as the 'organ of the historical' – to accept one of the many possible versions of history.[32]

This understanding is paralleled by Nietzsche's solution to the total perspectivism he claimed. In the face of this perspectivism he postulated and approved a 'will to power' which might impose its vision. Such a will and power was to be the mode in which 'free, *very* free spirits' might become 'the poets of [their] lives.'[33]

At this point an important distinction can be made between

what might be called 'subjectivism' and subjectivity. A term coined by Michael Polanyi which can be of considerable use here is 'universal intent.'[34] Some statements are intended as purely subjective – 'I have a toothache.' Such statements are the targets of one facet of Wittgenstein's attack on private language. Subjectivity, or subjective appropriation, is on another level. Appropriated statements are made with universal intent; they are claimed to hold for everyone. This sort of claim cuts across the metaphysically generated distinction between subjective and objective typical of Logical Positivism.

It is worth noticing that both Kierkegaard's 'passion' and Wittgenstein's 'ethical' are intensely individual, even personal categories. The existential dimension has a great importance in their ways of thinking. Wittgenstein expresses this in the *Investigations*, when he says that the 'real discovery is the one that makes *me* capable of stopping doing philosophy when I want to.'[35]

This existential bias shows itself repeatedly. The most obvious indication of it is the reduplicative address to the individual reader. Kierkegaard conceived religious communication to be as important for the speaker as for the hearer; in the case of his speaking it undoubtedly was. But this importance could only be an importance for the individual. Wittgenstein's later philosophy is in the first person. It reflects his own struggles, and the expected struggles of those who attempt to follow him.[36] Only an individual decision can end the philosophical process, as he suggests in *On Certainty*: 'I act with *complete* certainty. But this certainty is my own.'[37]

An additional perspective on this existential dimension can be gained by relating Kierkegaard's and Wittgenstein's understanding to the solution proposed by Polanyi. The only source for negation of doubt in his opinion – and in keeping with his conclusion he stresses that it is his opinion, albeit with universal intent – is a personal form of commitment.[38] This is what Kierkegaard calls the 'truth *for me*' which '*must come alive in me.*' What gives this commitment significance is Kierkegaard's intention to shout his resolution to everyone he meets.[39]

The existential and personal bias also shows itself in the switch from the emphasis on correct theories in the traditional fields of philosophy and theology to the examination of possible 'forms of life' or 'stages on life's way' and their consequences. Such a shift suggests a radical change in the place of philosophical thinking in life. Rather than a formal and foundational discipline, which sets the boundaries of possibility – in addition to metaphysics, normative ethics comes to mind – it becomes a tool to be used in the clarification of the problems that arise inevitably in life. It remains 'ethical' in a broad sense, but ceases to be 'normative.'

As such, while it may remain a technical discipline – in the sense that a certain kind of critical and analogical thinking is involved, and there will always be more and less skillful practitioners – philosophy ought not to remain a domain reserved for professionals. (This reflects Wittgenstein's comment that there must be room for the 'skillful' as well as the 'great.')

In fact it cannot remain so reserved, because a scheme in which the individual's appropriation plays such an essential part reduces the importance of technical 'understanding' significantly.

Both thinkers suggest that some other concerns must be ultimate. This is the most important relativising of the western 'understanding.' In an epistemological dimension, personal appropriation is paramount. There is also for both authors an 'ethical' or 'religious' dimension. This dimension is masked by the personal in such a way that it is very difficult to discuss. But clearly both intend their work to lead to a re-conception of the world in these terms. Certainly it had that effect in their own lives.

Three categories mark the road to continuation of philosophy in the mode of Kierkegaard and Wittgenstein. One of these categories is that of 'reduplication.' As mentioned in chapter 2, the lowest level of reduplication in the works is the combination of the 'theoretical' and 'specific' levels in such a way that most remarks bear on both at once. Another level, at which the two authors explicitly call for reduplication, is the requirement that the individual reader reduplicate in her life the specific 'theoretical' understanding gained from reading. This dimension forms a link between the level of communication and the final dimension in which reduplication is called for – the level of personal life. The individual is required to live authentically and passionately. She is informed by the form of life chosen.

The second category is that of the individual. In chapter 3 it has been shown how the individual plays an essential part in the understanding of the world within individual language-games and across the boundaries between them. In the present context it will suffice to remember that the philosophical is in many respects a language-game like any other. The philosophy student's role must be like that of the listener in a devotional address, and the lecturer's like that of the preacher.

The final category is that of the task. This category has multiple implications. It is of course connected to the individual – a task is only a task for an existing individual. It is also connected to the idea of reduplication: this is an important part of the task. But the most important connection of the idea of the task is an ethical one. It is in the ethical sphere that the individual is fundamentally autonomous from the social requirements of language-games. 'The ethical' is of course in one sense a language-game. But the process of accepting language-games which constitutes the ethical game can only operate at the individual level. Kierkegaard's 'leap of faith' is an ethical decision in this sense. It is a decision made by the individual in despite (not to say in defiance) of the lack of public information. Choices between language-games are only possible in this mode, since the internal logic of a game precludes such a choice. The material in chapter 4 gives a more extended analysis of this point.

This willfully uninformed choice is the ultimate 'relativising' of the language-game of understanding. As against the paradigm of objective conformity to the 'truth,' it represents an ideal of passionate personal justification. As against the mechanical conception of proof (borrowed from the scientific method and formal logic), it suggests the need to accept on inadequate evidence – daring to be formed, to reduplicate the movements suggested. While at an everyday level (as explicated in the 'Private Language Argument') the criterion of certainty is simple inability to doubt, at the level of transition or tension between games, the criterion is willful conquest of doubt. This is where Polanyi refers to 'commitment,' and Nietzsche to 'will to power.'

Kierkegaard's understanding of this feature is expressed in the statement that 'subjectivity is truth, subjectivity is reality':[40] subjective existence is the mode of fullest actualization. In a journal entry, he says that

> the remarkable thing is that there is a How with the characteristic that when the How is scrupulously rendered the What is also given, that this is the How of 'faith.' Right here, at its very maximum, inwardness is shown to be objectivity.[41]

Appropriation, which might seem to promote the ultimate in relativity, becomes the approach to ultimate reality.

The remaining task is to suggest a direction in which the spirit of Kierkegaard and Wittgenstein can be reduplicated in the extension of philosophy and theology. The danger in this task is that there are certainly many methods and constructs in their work which could have broader application.

For example, the idea of perspectivism and the address to the individual has considerable consequences for the way in which philosophy is done. Traditional philosophical arguments are intended to be fully rational. But at some point there is a threshold of acceptance at which the argument is enthymematic. A good example of this threshold is Aquinas's repeated comment, 'and this thing every man admits to be God.' If indeed every man admitted this point, at least one of the Five Ways must succeed. But in fact this is the very place at which the way swings off. It is quite possible that a difference in perspective may lead to the reader following the argument perfectly, but denying that it does in fact prove what is claimed.[42]

The address to the individual shows its value at precisely this sticky point. An explicit recognition of the problem of differing perspectives must result in the ground of argument being changed. Rather than stressing the factual content, the argument will attempt to persuade. Thus one practical advantage of the 'new way' is that a point at which leverage needs to be applied has been found.

Another technical advance which can be derived from the two authors' work is the understanding of various conceptual systems as more or less intertwined 'stages,' 'language-games' and 'forms of life.' *Pace* Alasdair MacIntyre, this understanding can be used as a conceptual scheme to help clarify the confusing issues of inter-societal understanding in a way sensitive to all sides. It might also have profitable application in the philosophy of physical science. The problem of progress addressed by Kuhn and others seems particularly susceptible of such an analysis. Polanyi's work has already followed a similar direction.[43]

A field which might benefit from the conception of language-games is Biblical hermeneutics. One application which has already been made is based on the idea of multiple grammars. Anthony Thiselton suggests that at least three different grammatical levels

115

are represented in Paul's letters. He remarks that some of Paul's distinctions are founded on 'universal' grammar – if anything is true, they are. Others 'express the attitude of a particular tradition.' They are foundational for that tradition, though perhaps not clear within some other traditions.[44] Thiselton suggests that a third class of grammatical remarks made by Paul have an intention which Kierkegaard would call 'maieutic'; they suggest new pictures or call new attention (positive or negative) to the old.[45]

These technical advances, while interesting and useful, are nevertheless not the reduplication of Kierkegaard or of Wittgenstein. They can be appropriated without being appropriated. They argue for or about a new way of seeing, without arguing *from* such a new way. In order to be existentially appropriated, they would need to be grounded in the new spirit both authors propose. At that point, they might almost be discarded as methods without being the less appropriated.

The fundamental difference in philosophy proposed by the two authors is the emphasis on the individual's reduplication of itself and of the world. This emphasis is perfectly clearly presented by Kierkegaard: 'The self is a relation that relates itself to itself.'[46] The emphasis in this relation is not on either term being related, but on the quality of the relation itself. The locus of subjective individuality is not placed in the existing self or the ideal self, but rather in the 'positive third term' – the constant task of integration. Thus even at the basic level of self-constitution, reduplication is present.

In the *Tractatus*, Wittgenstein presents a similar position in the puzzling guise of an approval of solipsism. But Wittgenstein's approval of solipsism's basic position is not nearly as puzzling when seen in the light of Kierkegaard's remarks. The solipsist attempts to say what can only be shown: that 'the world is *my* world.'[47] This statement does not reflect any *fact* about 'the subject that thinks or entertains ideas'; Wittgenstein denies that there is any such 'thing' within the world.[48] Rather, the 'metaphysical subject' is the 'positive unity' (to use Kierkegaard's term) in the self's relation and bounding of the world. Only in its relational capacity does this self enter philosophy; only because 'the world is my world.'[49]

As the flow of chapter 3 has suggested, even in his later period Wittgenstein would still have accepted this part of the basic idea behind solipsism. Individuals and their actions are the only source of instantiation of language-games, which are fundamentally non-existent unless instantiated.

The 'new spirit' in philosophy would necessarily be involved with this relational self in two ways. It would of course involve an address to the individual self; only by addressing me can one alter *my* world. That such an alteration in the direction of address is part of the project proposed by Kierkegaard and Wittgenstein has been amply demonstrated above. But more important, the new spirit would be a new qualification of the relation which constitutes the individual self. Admitting Kierkegaard's claim that 'man is spirit,' the positing of a new spirit would actually be the positing of a new self. This new self would be one for which the world has 'waxed as a whole.' In Kierkegaard's terms, it would find a new grounding by which 'despair is completely rooted out.'[50]

Under such an active paradigm, philosophy could at most only be called a task. It could more profitably be called a tool in the service of a higher task. This 'higher' task is the task of life. Seeing the world aright is not a possible achievement of an article in a philosophical journal. Kierkegaard's dread of being turned into a 'paragraph in the universal system' by some assistant professor, and Wittgenstein's preference for the elimination of the need for philosophy over a continuation of his, are strong testimonials for this reduplicative reading.

Philosophy's progress then becomes a continual process of self-transcendence. But, like the Knight of Faith, the philosopher who does not 'remain standing' at philosophy is nevertheless in a dialectical tension which finds him returning to philosophy often. The advantage gained is that this dialectical tension is no longer demonically driven from the side of philosophy – a philosophy which one cannot stop doing. Instead, the tension arises naturally from the circumstances of life.

The richness of life is also more available to philosophy on this model. The new balanced diet helps to eliminate the dangers of anorexia (as in Logical Positivism) and bulimia (as in MacIntyre's social science, which swallows the factual content of other worldviews whole, only to reject them utterly as unworthy). Such richness is amply demonstrated in the works of Bouwsma. There literary allusions and horrible puns rub shoulders with the most respectable philosophy. Nietzsche's omnivorous new ideal and his multiple 'masked' style also give some suggestion of this acceptance of the world's richness.

Ironically, by being thus relativised, the philosophical approach gains immeasurably in importance and in the scope of its action.

Chapter Six

NOW I CAN GO ON!

This study has reached the point at which, according to tradition, the conclusions reached ought to be presented. But it is particularly difficult to imagine 'presenting a conclusion' to a study of two figures who were concerned above all to keep their work from culminating in a 'result.' Wittgenstein once said of a student who declined to complete his dissertation that he should be given his doctorate for that act alone![1]

The hunger for results, for a 'contribution to scholarship,' derives in part from the usages of science. In the scientific scheme of factual investigation, a theory resulting from one's work is stated, and that theory constitutes one's contribution.

The work of both Kierkegaard and Wittgenstein is subversive of the scientific scheme. Each hoped to have made contributions. But a feature central to their projects, and thus one of their contributions, is the establishment of the possibility of contributing without presenting theoretical results.

If this possibility is to be realized, the reader must recognize a deep congruity between her task and that of the author. *Both* tasks are reinterpreted and considerably broadened.

One way of understanding the change in the author's task is to notice the transition from factual to conceptual investigations. This transition does not imply a lessening in the quantity of facts presented, but rather a shift in the use of these facts. They are no longer divisible into data and results. Instead they are presented as reminders, showings, and signposts in the indirect communication of conceptual clarifications.

The author does not superimpose theories (which claim to be results, newly created facts) on the world, thus solving larger factual problems. Instead he makes a perspicuous connection of the facts, working out how he is inclined to 'go on' conceptually, in a therapeutic attempt to *dissolve* the particular problem at hand.

The reader's task also involves an attempt to 'go on.' The movements of the author are to be reduplicated. Reading becomes a training process. A successful communication would culminate in the reader's ability to continue as the author would in a variety of situations. Another level of success (quite foreign to theory-communication) might be reached when the reader convinced the author that another way of going on was preferable.

This understanding of the author and the reader as equals in conversation involves an appreciation for the immense power and complexity of language, for the nonetheless inexpressibly multi-faceted nature of the world, and for the individual who alone can make sense of it all.[2] At first glance, there appear to be firm boundaries between the works of Kierkegaard, the *Tractatus*, and the later writings of Wittgenstein. Each of these communications works from a different body of facts. But a deep respect for the place and power of the individual constitutes a strong bond between the works.

This respect and its ramifications are perhaps best shown in the lives of the two figures. They each made an effort to be readers as well as authors of their own works. They attempted reduplication of life into works, works into life. This attempt ought to be taken seriously as a part of their communication.

A new sense of the boundaries between Kierkegaard and the 'two Wittgensteins' would be a particularly appropriate contribution to the study of these two figures. Some of the most important objects of dissolution or reinterpretation for both Kierkegaard and Wittgenstein are boundaries of various kinds. This is one area in which the transition from the factual to the conceptual has great impact. Factual boundaries do not seem like good candidates for change. Conceptual boundaries are much more fluid. This is not to say that they are arbitrary; they are purposive, and purposes do not remain constant.

In fact, one individual may have multiple purposes at the same time – for example, an absolute relation to the absolute *telos* and a relative relation to relative ends. Both Kierkegaard and Wittgenstein spoke of the boundaries between schemes of thinking in ways which suggest that they conceived them as fluid and capable of superimposition.

This conception has many consequences for the study of Kierkegaard and Wittgenstein, and for larger philosophical and religious problems. The most immediate impact is that 'stages on life's way,' 'language-games' and 'forms of life' no longer need be thought of as metaphysical constructs. All were first of all heuristic or maieutic constructs. If they are to be accepted as more broadly useful ways of grasping the world and thus have continued life, they cannot be sclerosed into schemata of distinct regions, permanently separated by quasi-physical boundaries.

The implication of Kierkegaard and Wittgenstein in two general problems for philosophy and religion – fideism and relativism – depends on the sclerotic understanding of these constructs. The specific charge of fideism presupposes the understanding of 'reason' (perhaps 'factual' reason) as a self-contained system, which is opposable to the equally self-contained system of 'paradoxical religion.' In this scheme, one must be either a rational scientist or an irrational fideist.

The irony of this claim is that the very term 'paradox' implies the holding fast of the collision between reason and non-reason. In itself it denies the metaphysical boundary-scheme! It simply claims that neither is sufficient when the task is life. Both are essential, but in different ways corresponding to their different possibilities. They are essential to the individual. If they were not, the paradox would never arise.

A similar reminder is in order concerning the complaint of relativism. This complaint is usually advanced by western reason when it is frustrated by the inability to make adherents of other worldviews hew instantly to its line. The complaint of fideism is generalized into an accusation of general invincibility, the possibility of cross-worldview understanding is denied, and those who suggest validity for multiple self-consistent systems are convicted of having no values.

This problem can be more productively understood in the context of maieutic conceptual communication. Grasping the multiplicity of language-games within societies which are commonly understood as single units, and the participation of individuals in various language-games, both synchronically and diachronically, yields the beginning of a dissolution of the 'problem' of cultural relativism. The fact of participation in both religion and reason by individuals is one example of this multiplicity, as are such relatively simpler examples as the use of computers (and the allied technical knowledge) in the humanities. The idea of concentric accretions stands as a useful corrective to the scientific idea of linear additions.

A central feature of this new pattern is the 'task' or 'activity.' The appropriateness of concepts depends on the context. So noticing the *point* of actions becomes essential. There is a close relation between meaning and usage.

The 'absolutist' scientific view can be undercut by recalling the task-dependent multiple uses of such a simple term as 'exact.' Within one experiment, a scientist might note the duration of neural impulses in milliseconds and the duration of resulting activities in seconds. Neither standard of exactness would prevent the scientist from preparing a three-minute egg using a sandglass, or arriving for dinner 'fashionably late.' In each case she might have gotten the timing 'exactly right.' Exactness is a term of praise, and not a single standard.[3]

The appropriateness of concepts for their contexts (which is itself a thoroughly complex notion) can profitably be extended from such simple examples to complex social phenomena such as religion and even magic. Schemes of this sort, like the scientific project of 'understanding,' propose tasks and concepts of an overarching importance. But at this level too, the meaning of one's task can only become clear in the use made of it.

It is difficult to separate recommendations aimed at philosophers from the other aspects of the two authors' work. This difficulty is true to the multi-layered and recursive nature of their task. But one possible line for extension of the present study might be suggested.

Kierkegaard and Wittgenstein have attempted to re-conceptualize the appropriateness of certain activities for religious writers and philosophers, and their respective audiences. This new proposal opens up a connection between the two fields which may easily be productive for both. It remains for the connection to be continued by other writers, and appropriated by *their* audiences. Such a continuation in the conceptual spirit would be viewed as a success (or at least a non-failure) by each. At a minimum, they might hope that the friction between philosophical and religious thought could produce new insights. But this possibility can only come to fruition through an appreciation for the importance of several concepts common to the two authorships.

NOW I CAN GO ON!

The potential in this connection derives from the possibility of transition between two conceptual schemes. The chance to see the world differently is an important step on the road to seeing the world aright.

In such a transitional situation it would be inappropriate to demand objective conformity to established rules. The point of making connections between these two games lies precisely in the opportunity offered to re-examine the rules of each. In such a vulnerable situation, the emphasis must be on 'good will.'

What here supplements rule-following and requires the exercise of good will is the process which Wittgenstein called 'going on.' The potential to make various connections between various ideas is not even latent until it has been actively tested.

Most important, this entire process of connection is radically dependent on the perceptions and other deeds of individual existing human beings. Transitions can only be made by people; good will is a personal mode; only individuals can go on. Even one system is lifeless without active application. Surely the juxtaposition of two games can be made *clear* only if it has been made in the first place. 'Only in the stream of thought and life do words have meaning.' This is not a limitation of systems, but an invitation to life.

The hopes of this attempt to 'go on' in the way which Kierkegaard and Wittgenstein attempted and recommended are summed up in a remark Wittgenstein made in conversation with Drury:[4] 'Bach wrote on the title page of his *Orgelbuchlein*, "To the glory of the most high God, and that my neighbour may be benefited thereby." That is what I would have liked to say about my work.'

NOTES

INTRODUCTION

1 It is worth noting in this context that a recent multi-volume compilation of articles on Wittgenstein has in its composite index only one reference to Kierkegaard. The reference is to a footnote in an article by a European Wittgenstein scholar, who there issues a general denial that anything about Wittgenstein's methods or aims has any relation to Kierkegaard's project. (Joachim Schulte (1986) 'Wittgenstein and conservatism,' in *Ludwig Wittgenstein: Critical Assessments*, 4 vols, ed. Stuart Shanker, London: Croom Helm, 4:69n.)
2 Søren Kierkegaard (1962) *The Point of View for My Work as an Author: A Report to History*, trans. Walter Lowrie, New York: Harper Torchbooks, p. 6.
3 Ludwig Wittgenstein (1958) *Philosophical Investigations*, 3rd edn, trans. G. E. M. Anscombe, New York: Macmillan Publishing Co., §127.
4 Norman Malcolm (1984) *Ludwig Wittgenstein: A Memoir*, 2nd edn, New York: Oxford University Press, p. 69.
5 Søren Kierkegaard (1967–75) *Søren Kierkegaard's Journals and Papers*, 7 vols, ed. and trans. Howard V. Hong and Edna H. Hong, Bloomington, IN: Indiana University Press, §709 (X^4 A 596). (The number in parentheses is the standard reference to the entry, from the Danish edition of the *Papirer*.)
6 *Investigations*, §127.

1 RELEVANT BIOGRAPHY

1 G. H. von Wright (1974) Introduction to *Letters to Russell, Keynes and Moore*, by Ludwig Wittgenstein, Ithaca, NY: Cornell University Press, p. 1.
2 Ludwig Wittgenstein (1965) 'Wittgenstein's lecture on ethics,' *Philosophical Review* 74:4–5.
3 W. W. Bartley's infamous biography of 1973, *Wittgenstein* (Philadelphia, PA: J. B. Lippincott) attributes most if not all of this 'self-hatred' to the 'fact' that Wittgenstein was unhappily homosexual. The depth of his

despair and his conception of its overarching effect on his life and work suggest that Wittgenstein's moral condition could not have been *totally* determined by such a cause.

4 Norman Malcolm (1984) *Ludwig Wittgenstein: A Memoir*, 2nd edn, New York: Oxford University Press, p. 52.
5 Malcolm, *Memoir*, p. 98.
6 Malcolm, *Memoir*, p. 84.
7 Karl Britton (1967) 'Portrait of a philosopher,' in *Ludwig Wittgenstein: The Man and His Philosophy*, ed. K. T. Fann, New York: Dell, p. 60.
8 Hermine Wittgenstein (1981) 'My brother Ludwig,' in *Ludwig Wittgenstein: Personal Recollections*, ed. Rush Rhees, Totowa, NJ: Rowman & Littlefield, p. 5.
9 Malcolm, *Memoir*, p. 26.
10 Britton, 'Portrait,' p. 60.
11 Letter from Wittgenstein to Russell, dated 22.6.12., *Letters to Russell*, p. 10.
12 The phrase comes from Schopenhauer by way of M. O'C. Drury.
13 For example, see Malcolm, *Memoir*, p. 33.
14 Hermine Wittgenstein, 'My brother Ludwig,' p. 4.
15 According to Mrs Eccles, the wife of a fellow student. Reported by Wolfe Mays (1967) 'Recollections of Wittgenstein,' in *Ludwig Wittgenstein: The Man and His Philosophy*, p. 88.
16 On this point see B. F. McGuinness, editor's appendix to Paul Engelmann (1968) *Letters from Ludwig Wittgenstein, With a Memoir*, New York: Horizon Press, pp. 141–42.
17 Bartley, *Wittgenstein*, p. 126.
18 Loos 'once said to Wittgenstein: "You are me!"' Engelmann, *Letters*, p. 127.
19 Hermine Wittgenstein, 'Family recollections,' ch. VI, in Bernhard Leitner (1976) *The Architecture of Ludwig Wittgenstein*, New York: New York University Press, p. 23.
20 Quoted in Allan Janik and Stephen Toulmin (1973) *Wittgenstein's Vienna*, New York: Simon & Schuster, p. 208.
21 Malcolm, *Memoir*, p. 78.
22 Malcolm, *Memoir*, p. 60.
23 Maurice O'C. Drury (1981) 'Some notes on conversations with Wittgenstein,' in *Ludwig Wittgenstein: Personal Recollections*, p. 91.
24 Friedrich Waismann (1965) 'Notes on talks with Wittgenstein,' *Philosophical Review* 74:16. Wittgenstein's religious understanding (as far as he expressed it) will be discussed at greater length in chapter 4.
25 Maurice O'C. Drury (1981) 'Conversations with Wittgenstein,' in *Ludwig Wittgenstein: Personal Recollections*, pp. 112ff.
26 Drury, 'Conversations,' p. 130.
27 Drury, 'Some notes,' p. 109.
28 Reported by Mrs Bevan, the wife of the doctor in whose house Wittgenstein was staying. Malcolm, *Memoir*, p. 81.
29 Malcolm, *Memoir*, p. 81.
30 Engelmann, *Letters*, p. 79.

31 Søren Kierkegaard (1941) *Concluding Unscientific Postscript*, trans. David F. Swenson and Walter Lowrie, Princeton, NJ: Princeton University Press, p. 147; cf. pp. 365ff.
32 Another possible source of this orientation is Tolstoy. In 1915 Wittgenstein acquired his exposition of the Gospels. This work reflects Tolstoy's interest in the simple life as a religious duty; but if Wittgenstein's position was influenced by the work, it certainly could not have been *wholly* inspired by it. The sequence of his further acquaintance with Tolstoy is not clear.
33 Letter from Bertrand Russell to Lady Ottoline Morrell, December 20, 1919. In *Letters to Russell*, p. 82.
34 See for instance *Postscript*, pp. 359ff. Ironically, the *Postscript* is attributed to a monastic pseudonym, Johannes Climacus.
35 H. D. P. Lee (1979) 'Wittgenstein 1929–1931,' *Philosophy* 54:218.
36 Waismann, 'Notes on talks,' p. 13. Compare Søren Kierkegaard (1985) *Philosophical Fragments*, trans. Howard V. Hong and Edna H. Hong, Princeton, NJ: Princeton University Press, p. 37. Wittgenstein rejected this formulation only a year later (Waismann, p. 16); but this rejection seems to be an instance of the 'later' Wittgenstein failing fully to understand the possibilities of the 'earlier' position – of which more in subsequent chapters.
37 Ludwig Wittgenstein (1967) *Lectures and Conversations on Aesthetics, Psychology and Religious Belief*, ed. Cyril Barrett, Berkeley, CA: University of California Press, p. 70. (In this work square brackets represent composite collations and editorial guesswork.) Wittgenstein's understanding of the connection of 'proof' and 'picture' is explored in chapter 4.
38 Søren Kierkegaard (1987) *Either/Or*, 2 vols, trans. Howard V. Hong and Edna H. Hong, Princeton, NJ: Princeton University Press, II:266–70.
39 Drury, 'Some notes,' pp. 102–3.
40 O. K. Bouwsma (1986) *Wittgenstein: Conversations 1949–1951*, ed. J. L. Craft and R. E. Hustwit, Indianapolis, IN: Hackett Publishing Co., p. 46.
41 Malcolm, *Memoir*, p. 106. Malcolm indicates that Wittgenstein *had* read the *Postscript* (p. 60).
42 Ludwig Wittgenstein (1980) *Culture and Value*, trans. Peter Winch, Chicago, IL: University of Chicago Press, pp. 31e–32e. (In references to this posthumous collection, the date given is the year in which Wittgenstein composed the entry.)
43 *Culture and Value* p. 38e (1940).
44 Søren Kierkegaard (1978) *Two Ages*, trans. Howard V. Hong and Edna H. Hong, Princeton, NJ: Princeton University Press, pp. 61, 68.
45 Søren Kierkegaard (1955) *On Authority and Revelation: The Book on Adler*, trans. Walter Lowrie, Princeton, NJ: Princeton University Press, pp. 159–60.
46 Søren Kierkegaard (1971) *Christian Discourses*, trans. Walter Lowrie, Princeton, NJ: Princeton University Press, p. 11.

47 *Culture and Value* p. 53e (1946).
48 Janik and Toulmin, *Wittgenstein's Vienna*, p. 24.
49 K. E. Tranøy (1976) 'Wittgenstein in Cambridge 1949–51, some personal recollections,' in *Essays on Wittgenstein in Honor of G. H. von Wright*, Amsterdam: North Holland Publishing Co., pp. 12–13.
50 Walter Lowrie (1962) *Kierkegaard*, New York: Harper Torchbooks, pp. 10–11.
51 Walter Lowrie's assertion that Kierkegaard often thought of himself under the name 'Ludwig' is surely worth neither less nor more than a footnote – which is in fact what he accords it. See his note to Søren Kierkegaard (1941) *Judge for Yourselves!*, trans. Walter Lowrie, Princeton, NJ: Princeton University Press, p. 194.
52 It must be noted that this failure to travel was not due to financial problems; Kierkegaard, like Wittgenstein, had a rich inheritance (and unlike Wittgenstein he did not hesitate to spend it on luxuries). Nor was it due to any social constraints; others in his circle, such as Hans Christian Andersen, travelled widely in Europe. But Denmark suited Kierkegaard, and travel did not.
53 Søren Kierkegaard (1962) *The Point of View for My Work as an Author: A Report to History*, trans. Walter Lowrie, New York: Harper Torchbooks, p. 100.
54 'For that I myself possess a more exact and purely personal interpretation of my life is a matter of course.' *The Point of View*, p. 98n.
55 Lowrie's works could perhaps be called an 'indirect communication' insofar as he allows Kierkegaard to say what Lowrie wants(!). His method of working certainly is that of 'assembling reminders.'
56 Søren Kierkegaard (1943) *Edifying Discourses*, 4 vols, trans. David F. Swenson and Lillian Marvin Swenson, Minneapolis, MN: Augsburg Publishing House, 1:3,5.
57 Søren Kierkegaard, *Søren Kierkegaard's Journals and Papers*, 7 vols, ed. and trans. Howard V. Hong and Edna H. Hong, Bloomington, IN: Indiana University Press, §5874 (VII^{1}A 5).
58 *The Point of View*, p. 76.
59 *Journals and Papers*, §5430 (II A 805). Lowrie dates the 'earthquake' to 1830.
60 *Journals and Papers*, §5431 (II A 806).
61 It is perhaps fortunate that W. W. Bartley has not written a biography of Kierkegaard; surely the talk of a 'thorn in the flesh,' causing sin- and guilt-consciousness, and which he once asked his physician about, to see if 'the discordancy between the bodily and the psychical in my constitution could be removed so that I might realize the universal [i.e. marriage]' (Lowrie, *Kierkegaard*, p. 405), is excellent *prima facie* evidence of Kierkegaard's homosexuality!
62 Lowrie, *Kierkegaard*, p. 239.
63 Søren Kierkegaard (1983) *Repetition*, trans. Howard V. Hong and Edna H. Hong, Princeton, NJ: Princeton University Press, pp. 142–5.
64 *Journals and Papers*, §6388 (X^1 A 266).
65 *The Point of View*, pp. 105–38.

66 *Journals and Papers*, §1959 (X³ A 413).
67 *Journals and Papers*, §5368 (II A 347).
68 *Journals and Papers*, §5324 (II A 228).
69 *Authority and Revelation*, pp. 118–20. Kierkegaard published only an abridgement of this work which did not mention Adler. This passage is from the few pages Kierkegaard added when he published the brief discussion 'Of the difference between a genius and an apostle.'
70 Although no one would deny (given their respective contexts) that Kierkegaard's was a Christian religious experience and Wittgenstein's was not, it is interesting to note that neither this report of the aftermath of an experience nor Constantin Constantius's parody of mystical experience (*Repetition*, p. 173) mention any specifically Christian *content*.
71 *The Point of View*, pp. 49–50.
72 A 'Knight of Faith' (in 'Religiousness B') ought to have been able to be at once married and 'in the service of the Higher.' So Kierkegaard's break with Regine confirms the state of his religiousness.
73 *The Point of View*, p. 75.
74 *The Point of View*, p. 6.
75 *Postscript*, p. 132n.
76 *The Point of View*, pp. 71–2.
77 *Repetition*, p. 135.
78 *Journals and Papers*, §6192 (IX A 142).
79 Malcolm, *Memoir*, p. 83.
80 Wittgenstein did not think of this moral demand as a constraint; even under the burden of his incomplete task, he still had a 'wonderful life.' Kierkegaard's description of the Knight of Faith's freedom from worldly burdens comes to mind. So does Wittgenstein's house, with its strange combination of strict design and free feeling.

2 METHODOLOGY

1 This is certainly not to imply that there is no connection between the two periods. See chapters 4 and 5 for a fuller exploration of this connection.
2 Ludwig Wittgenstein (1958) *Philosophical Investigations*, 3rd edn, trans. G. E. M. Anscombe, New York: Oxford University Press, §109.
3 Søren Kierkegaard (1962) *The Point of View for My Work as an Author: A Report to History*, trans. Walter Lowrie, New York: Harper Torchbooks, p. 6 (and many other references in his works).
4 Ludwig Wittgenstein (1960) *The Blue and Brown Books*, 2nd edn, New York: Harper Torchbooks, p. 64.
5 Ludwig Wittgenstein (1974) *Tractatus Logico-Philosophicus*, trans. D. F. Pears and B. F. McGuinness, New York: The Humanities Press, §4.112, §4.114–§4.115.
6 Søren Kierkegaard (1985) *Philosophical Fragments*, trans. Howard V. Hong and Edna H. Hong, Princeton, NJ: Princeton University Press, p. 37. Compare Moore's report on Wittgenstein: 'He said . . . that we had to follow a certain instinct which leads us to ask certain

questions, though we don't even understand what these questions mean; that our asking them results from "a vague mental uneasiness," like that which leads children to ask "Why?"....' From G. E. Moore (1954–5) 'Wittgenstein's lectures in 1930–33,' *Mind* 63–64, no. 253, p. 27.
7 *The Point of View*, p. 6.
8 Søren Kierkegaard (1941) *Concluding Unscientific Postscript*, trans. David F. Swenson and Walter Lowrie, Princeton, NJ: Princeton University Press, p. 178n.
9 *The Point of View*, p. 59. In fact, Kierkegaard's polemic is redoubled, since New Testament Christianity is already a polemical lifestyle, established over against the world. See Søren Kierkegaard (1967–75) *Søren Kierkegaard's Journals and Papers*, 7 vols, ed. and trans. Howard V. Hong and Edna H. Hong, Bloomington, IN: Indiana University Press, §3336 (XI^1 A 156).
10 Søren Kierkegaard (1968) *The Concept of Irony, with Constant Reference to Socrates*, trans. Lee M. Capel, Bloomington, IN: Indiana University Press, p. 279.
11 *Investigations*, §127.
12 *Tractatus*, §4.1212.
13 Paul L. Holmer (1980) 'Wittgenstein: "saying" and "showing",' *Neue Zeitschrift für Systematische Theologie und Religionsphilosophie* 22:224.
14 *Investigations*, §1.
15 *Investigations*, §119.
16 *Investigations*, §499.
17 *Postscript*, p. 107.
18 Paul L. Holmer (1955) 'Kierkegaard and religious propositions,' *Journal of Religion* 35:135.
19 *Postscript*, pp. 164–7.
20 Moore, 'Wittgenstein's lectures,' 253:26–7.
21 Holmer, 'Wittgenstein: "saying" and "showing",' p. 224.
22 This example is mentioned in *Investigations*, §144; a longer explanation is given in Ludwig Wittgenstein (1970) *Zettel*, trans. G. E. M. Anscombe, Berkeley, CA: University of California Press, §461.
23 *Investigations*, §121.
24 Ludwig Wittgenstein (1979) *Remarks on Frazer's 'Golden Bough,'* trans. Rush Rhees, Atlantic Highlands, NJ: Humanities Press, p. 1e.
25 *The Point of View*, p. 27.
26 Ludwig Wittgenstein (1969) *On Certainty*, trans. Denis Paul and G. E. M. Anscombe, New York: Harper Torchbooks, p. 2e.
27 Maurice O'C. Drury (1981) 'Some notes on conversations with Wittgenstein,' in *Ludwig Wittgenstein: Personal Recollections*, ed. Rush Rhees, Totowa, NJ: Rowman & Littlefield, p. 93.
28 Ludwig Wittgenstein (1979) 'Letters to Ludwig von Ficker,' trans. Bruce Gillette; in *Wittgenstein: Sources and Perspectives*, ed. C. G. Luckhardt, Ithaca, NY: Cornell University Press, p. 92.
29 'Letters to Ficker,' pp. 94–5. The negative part of Wittgenstein's method is clearly reminiscent of the *via negativa* of theology. But I know

of no evidence to settle the question whether he had studied the classic sources in this area.

30 Wittgenstein's complaint about Kierkegaard's prolixity is worth recalling here. He was 'most likely to agree' (he *did* agree, by his own statement) with the goal of the project, but just this agreement could make him impatient with it, since it was not pitched at his level.

31 The gap between derivation and final form implies a danger for the author. He might lose track of the derivation, and thus later be at a loss to explain just what the point of each remark was. Indeed this seems to have been the case with Wittgenstein and the *Tractatus*. During 1929, Frank Ramsey discussed some points in this work with him. He admitted 'more than once' to having forgotten the exact meaning of statements. (Reported by Moore, 'Wittgenstein's lectures,' 249:3.) This is of course not to suggest that Wittgenstein later had trouble with the central concepts of the *Tractatus*; but the terse propositions are so tightly packed with meaning, derived from a long discourse and a complex context, that it would be surprising if he could unpack them exactly as originally intended.

32 *Investigations*, p. ix^c.

33 *Investigations*, §133.

34 A recent book by S. Stephen Hilmy (1987) *The Later Wittgenstein*, Oxford: Basil Blackwell, contains an extended discussion of the question whether the aphoristic style of the *Investigations* was intentional (pp. 15–25). Hilmy's conclusion is that Wittgenstein did want to write a 'normal' book, and that – no matter how complex the phenomena under discussion – the burden of the *Investigations* could in principle have been expressed in such a book. Nevertheless, the 'assembled' style does lend itself to the presentation of an assemblage of reminders. It certainly was Wittgenstein's working style.

35 *Journals and Papers*, §649 (VIII^2 B 81), pp. 269, 272.

36 *Journals and Papers*, §650 (VIII^2 B 82).

37 *Tractatus*, pp. 3, 5.

38 *Tractatus*, §6.13.

39 Unlike logic, valuations of the world can nevertheless change. This is an important difference! (In the *Investigations*, logic has the same status as values: 'standing fast' yet without metaphysical necessity.)

40 *Postscript*, p. 87.

41 *Tractatus*, §6.13, §6.421.

42 The fact that the essential parts of the *Tractatus* system are *not* self-containing (that nonsense has at least a maieutic use) ought to have been a clue to the positivists that their idea of a self-containing verificationism would turn out to be futile.

43 *Tractatus*, §6.54.

44 For example, *Investigations*, §128. Whether this position is in agreement with the *Tractatus* position or not is a nice question – since there theses were advanced, but only as a temporary scaffolding around the putatively self-supporting crystalline reality. (Shades of Kierkegaard's critique of the systematists who build palaces and dwell in hovels!)

45 Ludwig Wittgenstein (1979) *Remarks on Frazer's 'Golden Bough,'* trans. Rush Rhees, Atlantic Highlands, NJ: Humanities Press, p. 9e. Compare *Investigations*, §122.
46 *Investigations*, §123.
47 *Investigations*, §255. Kierkegaard says of 'the sickness unto death' that it nevertheless does not result in death, but continues indefinitely. How like Wittgenstein's philosophical sickness, which consists in being unable to stop philosophizing!
48 *Investigations*, §133.
49 *Investigations*, §109.
50 *Investigations*, §111. Edwards cites the discussion of 'nobody on the road' from *Through the Looking-Glass* as an example of an extended grammatical joke. See James C. Edwards (1982) *Ethics Without Philosophy: Wittgenstein and the Moral Life*, Tampa, FL: University Presses of Florida, pp. 120–1.
51 Norman Malcolm (1984) *Ludwig Wittgenstein: A Memoir*, 2nd edn, New York: Oxford University Press, pp. 27–8.
52 *Investigations*, §260. The point is that there is no room for such an external category as 'belief' here. (See chapter 3.) One recent commentator who has noticed Wittgenstein's use of sarcasm is Fergus Kerr. There are several references in his (1986) *Theology After Wittgenstein*, Oxford: Basil Blackwell.
53 *Investigations*, §464.
54 *Investigations*, §38.
55 *Investigations*, §664.
56 An excellent discussion of the uses of 'grammar' in the later philosophy is Debra Aidun (1982) 'Wittgenstein, philosophical method and aspect-seeing,' *Philosophical Investigations* 5:106–15. The puzzlement expressed by Moore in his 'Wittgenstein's lectures' is also very instructive about the unusual nature of Wittgenstein's use of this term.
57 *Investigations*, §254. 'I am inclined to say . . .' is a common expression in the later works and notes.
58 *Remarks on Frazer's 'Golden Bough,'* p. 9e.
59 At least, this is true in my experience. Wittgenstein uses the similar example of ability to continue a series. Many of the variety of possible ways of getting the next number in an algebraic series suggested in *Investigations*, §151 have parallels in the ways one might attempt to solve a crossword.
60 *Investigations*, p. 193e.
61 He also speaks of rousing traditional Christian theological concepts from their 'enchanted sleep,' restoring their 'lost power and meaning' *Journals and Papers*, §4774 (II A 110), §5181 (I A 328); cf. notes on 'Theologians, theology,' 4:737.
62 *Investigations*, p. x^e.
63 *Tractatus*, p. 3.
64 Søren Kierkegaard (1948) *Purity of Heart is To Will One Thing*, trans. Douglas V. Steere, New York: Harper Torchbooks, pp. 177ff.
65 *Journals and Papers*, §6700 (X^3 A 628).

66 Gregor Malantschuk, notes to 'Individual' in *Journals and Papers*, 2:597–8.
67 *The Point of View*, second note on 'The individual,' p. 124.
68 *The Point of View*, first note on 'The individual,' p. 110.
69 *The Point of View*, second note on 'The individual,' pp. 128–36.
70 *The Concept of Irony*, pp. 213–14.
71 'Letters to Ficker,' p. 92.
72 Søren Kierkegaard (1962) *Of the Difference Between a Genius and an Apostle*, trans. Alexander Dru, New York: Harper Torchbooks, p. 96.
73 For instance, see Ludwig Wittgenstein (1967) *Lectures and Conversations on Aesthetics, Psychology and Religious Belief*, ed. Cyril Barrett, Berkeley, CA: University of California Press, p. 48.
74 For example in Moore, 'Wittgenstein's lectures,' 253:19–20.
75 *Lectures and Conversations*, p. 28.
76 Quoted in Hilmy, *The Later Wittgenstein*, p. 21.
77 See Hilmy, *The Later Wittgenstein*, pp. 10–13, for a discussion of the dangers inherent in such a 'hypertextual' or 'radically contextual' interpretation of Wittgenstein's work.

3 PROBLEMS OF INTERPRETATION

1 Wittgenstein uses the concept 'game' to demonstrate the idea of 'family resemblance,' so of course the counter-example of solitaire or 'patience' comes to mind. But – to ask a Wittgensteinian question – why do we admit of the idea of 'cheating' at solitaire?
2 Ludwig Wittgenstein (1970) *Zettel*, trans. G. E. M. Anscombe, Berkeley, CA: University of California Press, §458.
3 Compare the status of logical and ethical statements in Wittgenstein's (1974) *Tractatus Logico-Philosophicus*, trans. D. F. Pears and B. F. McGuinness, New York: The Humanities Press. There 'nothing can be said' owing to the framework nature of these fields (and not, as the positivists would have it, because something fails to exist).
4 Ludwig Wittgenstein (1980) *Culture and Value*, trans. Peter Winch, Chicago, IL: University of Chicago Press, p. 9e. This note was made in 1931, well before the *Investigations* had reached even preliminary form, and the conception carries through in the various 'later' works.
5 Ludwig Wittgenstein (1958) *Philosophical Investigations*, 3rd edn, trans. G. E. M. Anscombe, New York: Macmillan Publishing Co., §247.
6 This sequence also can be understood in connection with the material about private language learning – the 'baby Crusoe' debate. That is a relatively separate strand, having more to do with the section on rules and going on.
7 The index of the *Investigations* lists ten separate phenomena which are explicitly claimed not to be mental processes! In this connection see also chapter 7 of Norman Malcolm (1986) *Nothing is Hidden*, New York: Basil Blackwell.
8 *Investigations*, §260.

9 *Investigations*, §288.
10 *Investigations*, §289. (An anti-positivist statement if ever there was one!)
11 *Zettel*, §472. In this entry and §488, Wittgenstein makes an attempt at writing down some of what 'we all know' about the use of psychological terms.
12 *Investigations*, §293.
13 *Investigations*, §307.
14 On this point see for instance G. E. Moore (1954–5) 'Wittgenstein's lectures in 1930–33,' *Mind* 249:6–9.
15 *Investigations*, §304. See also S. Stephen Hilmy (1987) *The Later Wittgenstein*, Oxford: Basil Blackwell, ch. II.
16 The 'definition' of meaning as use is given in *Investigations*, §43. But the German phrase which has been translated as 'it can be defined thus' is '*dieses Wort so erklären.*' Wittgenstein is not *defining* 'meaning,' but *explicating* the employment, or use (*Benützung*), of the word. The model of definition is precisely what he is rejecting, and it would be horribly ironic to try to define it out of existence!
17 *Zettel*, §273. Compare §606.
18 Anyone who believes in human free will must apparently admit some non-physical causality in human thinking. (Wittgenstein goes so far as to imply that 'causal efficacy' is a concept that does not apply in the human mind.)
   This suggestion also has ramifications for artificial intelligence research. If the human mind does not function causally, then one could not make a 'thinking machine' which duplicated its processes. (But that would not show that there could be no mechanical creation which behaved with enough of a family resemblance to 'intelligence' that we would wish to extend the term to include it.)
19 J. F. M. Hunter (1968) 'Forms of life in Wittgenstein's *Philosophical Investigations*,' *American Philosophical Quarterly* 5:4:233–43.
20 See Hilmy, *The Later Wittgenstein*, pp. 179–84, for a representative sample.
21 Peter Winch (1979) 'Understanding a primitive society,' in *Rationality*, ed. Bryan R. Wilson, Oxford: Basil Blackwell, pp. 107–11.
22 Hilmy, *The Later Wittgenstein*, p. 189.
23 *Investigations*, §65. Cf. Ludwig Wittgenstein (1960) *The Blue and Brown Books*, 2nd edn, New York: Harper Torchbooks, p. 81.
24 *Investigations*, §23.
25 *Investigations*, §373; compare *Zettel*, §717.
26 *Investigations*, p. 226e.
27 *Zettel*, §173. The thought is expressed many times in similar words.
28 The line comes from Goethe's *Faust*, part I. It appears in a note, written in 1937, and published in *Culture and Value*, p. 31e; and again in Wittgenstein's (1969) *On Certainty*, trans. Denis Paul and G. E. M. Anscombe, New York: Harper Torchbooks, §402, written in 1951. It also appears, in a remarkably different context, as the final phrase of Freud's *Totem and Taboo* (1913).

29 Again see Norman Malcolm's comments in chapter 8 of *Nothing is Hidden* (1986), New York: Basil Blackwell.
30 Alasdair MacIntyre, 'Is understanding religion compatible with believing?,' in *Rationality*, pp. 62–77. Sociological investigation of other cultures is of course not the same problem as investigation of religion by non-believers. But the analogies between these two games are fairly close, and there is general agreement that the comparison is valid.

  How one understands this argument depends largely on the scope one gives to the two concepts 'language-game' and 'form of life.' MacIntyre makes Christianity a totally different form of life from Western science, so he can claim there is no contact at all. On the other hand, his principle interlocutor, Peter Winch, argues that even Nuer religion is merely a different language-game within a 'limiting' common form of life, that of 'humanity.' (See Winch, 'Understanding a primitive society.')

  Winch's view is closer to that suggested in the discussion above, though both suffer from the tendency to see the two concepts as denoting objective facts, rather than suggesting fruitful ways of seeing.
31 On the possibility that such investigations could make us understand the historical development – and the question whether this matters to the importance of the beliefs – see Wittgenstein's (1979) *Remarks on Frazer's 'Golden Bough*,' trans. Rush Rhees, Atlantic Highlands, NJ: Humanities Press, especially pp. 8e and 16e.
32 The idea also has the interesting corollary that Western scientists (who believe in their disciplines) could never understand what they are doing!
33 '(The philosopher is not a citizen of any community of ideas. That is what makes him into a philosopher.)' *Zettel*, §455.
34 Wittgenstein's 'tip of the hat' to religion is another example of such an opening. In this connection it is also worth recalling Malcolm's idea that 'there was in him the *possibility* of religion.' Kierkegaard's ideas on 'paradox' in religion, which relate here, will be explored in the next chapter.
35 *Investigations*, §23.
36 *Investigations*, §201.
37 David Pears has an interesting perspective on Wittgenstein's attempts to keep philosophy separate from science. See his (1986) *Ludwig Wittgenstein*, Cambridge, MA: Harvard University Press, pp. 179–98.
38 The multi-layered nature of Wittgenstein's analysis is again evident here. The deed which shows understanding – the 'seeing' – can only be done by people, not philosophical sayings. See chapter 2.
39 Kierkegaard makes a similar point concerning the difficulty, which presupposes the possibility, of living in two spheres. 'Diplomats and police agents' are his examples. (Søren Kierkegaard (1941) *Concluding Unscientific Postscript*, trans. David F. Swenson and Walter Lowrie, Princeton, NJ: Princeton University Press, p. 365.) According to him, it is the Christian's task *constantly* to live in two spheres, maintaining an

absolute relation to the absolute *telos* and a relative relation to relative ends.
40 *On Certainty*, §174.
41 In fact, this edition has recently been available in mass-market bookstores, with a blurb describing it as 'one of the greatest fictional seductions'!
42 The 'system' of the Kierkegaardian stages has actually been displayed in chart form on the endpapers of a book.
43 While Wittgenstein was primarily concerned with classifying the possibilities of such a scheme, though he worked with it too, Kierkegaard used the scheme – though he classified parts of it too.
44 Henry Allison (1967) 'Christianity and nonsense,' *Review of Metaphysics* 20:432–60.
45 For instance, see Alistair McKinnon (1967) 'Kierkegaard: "paradox" and irrationalism,' *Journal of Existentialism* (Spring).
46 *Postscript*, p. 504.
47 Compare *Investigations*, §252.
48 *Postscript*, p. 86.
49 Here Wittgenstein's emphasis is in the opposite direction, although he notes the same phenomena as does Kierkegaard. Wittgenstein stresses that 'well-foundedness' is not an everyday criterion; thus everyday life is secure. Kierkegaard's emphasis on this point is designed to gain a foothold whereby a transition *away* from everyday life might be suggested (as well as to deny 'scientific' analysis its counterclaims).

There is also some question as to the compatibility of Kierkegaard's term and category 'appropriation-*process*' with Wittgenstein's understanding of the nature of an ability (which is mostly latent). Some part of the resolution of this problem will be undertaken in the next chapter.

Kierkegaard's analysis here appears to depend on a metaphysics which Wittgenstein would repudiate. His remarks in *Zettel*, §59ff. point out the dangers in 'this comparison: a man makes his appearance – an event makes its appearance. As if an event now stood in readiness before the door of reality and were then to make its appearance in reality – like coming into a room.' Further reflection on this difference of opinion might turn on the following points: 1) the *point* of Kierkegaard's discussion is not a metaphysical one; 2) the philosophical sections of the *Postscript* go beyond what 'can be said' existentially about reality; 3) there is a genuine difference here.
50 This attempt to guide oneself absolutely by a worldly scheme might be subsumed under the category 'ethical' – but it would still remain to show the philosophers that they ought to understand themselves under this category.
51 Compare Wittgenstein's statements on the point of the *Tractatus*.
52 Kierkegaard was well aware of the possibility that the meaning of words can be dependent on the game in which they are used. See chapters 4 and 5 for a fuller exploration of this awareness.
53 MacIntyre's analysis of Kierkegaard's 'ethical' in (1981) *After Virtue*, Notre Dame, IN: Notre Dame Press, pp. 38–43, does in fact take this

line. MacIntyre accuses Kierkegaard of hollow irrationality and pure relativism. (It is interesting to notice that MacIntyre's critiques of Kierkegaard and Wittgenstein are very similar.)
54 *Zettel*, §144. Wittgenstein appends the single word 'Theology' to this entry.
   The published translation, 'How *words* are understood is not told by words alone,' is a fine example of the applicability of this comment to translation. The doubling of *Wort* has been maintained, but the important difference in the sense is lost.
55 Søren Kierkegaard (1967–75) *Søren Kierkegaard's Journals and Papers*, 7 vols, ed. and trans. Howard V. Hong and Edna H. Hong, Bloomington, IN: Indiana University Press, §4056 (XI^2 A 106).
56 Søren Kierkegaard (1941) *Judge for Yourselves!*, trans. Walter Lowrie, Princeton, NJ: Princeton University Press, p. 207.
57 *Journals and Papers*, §1914 (X^4 A 556); *Judge for Yourselves!*, p. 207.
58 *Journals and Papers*, §1915 (X^4 A 626).
59 Søren Kierkegaard (1943) *Edifying Discourses*, 4 vols, trans. David F. Swenson and Lillian Marvin Swenson, Minneapolis, MN: Augsburg Publishing House, 2:7.
60 James 1:22 (Revised Standard Version).
61 *Edifying Discourses*, 2:84–5.
62 Kierkegaard's own 'maieutic' project has required that his inwardness – his ultimate intent – be hidden, but this is not the 'hidden inwardness' which he criticizes. His hiding was for a particular Christian purpose, and not for the sake of convenience. See *Journals and Papers*, §2125 (X^3 A 334).
63 Søren Kierkegaard (1962) *Works of Love*, trans. Howard V. Hong and Edna H. Hong, New York: Harper Torchbooks, pp. 26–7.
64 *Works of Love*, p. 23.
65 *Works of Love*, p. 33.
66 *Works of Love*, pp. 100–3. The parable is found in Matthew 21:28–31.
67 *Works of Love*, pp. 346–50.
68 For an extended explication of this idea as it applies to Kierkegaard's work in general, see O. K. Bouwsma (1984) 'Notes on Kierkegaard's "The Monstrous Illusion",' in *Without Proof or Evidence*, ed. J. L. Craft and R. E. Hustwit, Lincoln, NE: University of Nebraska Press, pp. 73–86.
69 The recognition of a Christian is made more problematic by the fact that it is not the Christian's purpose to be recognized as such. The exemplary 'Knight of Faith' in *Fear and Trembling* does not deal externally in specifically Christian words. The fulfiling of the law is not in terms of words, but of deeds informed by the Word.
70 Søren Kierkegaard (1983) *Fear and Trembling*, trans. Howard V. Hong and Edna H. Hong, Princeton, NJ: Princeton University Press, p. 37.
71 *Postscript*, pp. 438–9.
72 An obvious example is the vast number of volumes expended by religious mystics in the attempt to speak the ineffable and to aid others in experiencing it.
73 *Tractatus*, §6.54.

4 IMPLICATIONS FOR RELIGION

1 All of the references to religion are consistent in one respect: there is no indication of disdain for, or positivistic dismissal of religion. This fact comes as a surprise to many.
2 Søren Kierkegaard (1941) *Concluding Unscientific Postscript*, trans. David F. Swenson and Walter Lowrie, Princeton, NJ: Princeton University Press, p. 540.
3 Søren Kierkegaard (1967–75) *Søren Kierkegaard's Journals and Papers*, 7 vols, ed. and trans. Howard V. Hong and Edna H. Hong, Bloomington, IN: Indiana University Press, §4550 (X^2 A 299).
4 Ludwig Wittgenstein (1974) *Philosophical Grammar*, trans. Anthony Kenny, Oxford: Basil Blackwell, p. 370.
5 Previous considerations of Wittgenstein and religion have of course also entailed particular understandings of his methodology. A low estimation of the relevance of his work for religion would follow quite naturally from some of these understandings.
6 See chapter 2.
7 Ludwig Wittgenstein (1974) *Tractatus Logico-Philosophicus*, trans. D. F. Pears and B. F. McGuinness, New York: The Humanities Press, pp. 3, 5.
8 Ludwig Wittgenstein (1965) 'Wittgenstein's lecture on ethics,' *Philosophical Review* 74:8.
9 *Journals and Papers*, §96 (III A 235), §97 (V B 53:23).
10 *Tractatus*, §6.51; compare Ludwig Wittgenstein (1970) *Zettel*, trans. G. E. M. Anscombe, Berkeley, CA: University of California Press, § 458.
11 'Lecture on ethics,' p. 11.
12 Søren Kierkegaard (1980) *The Concept of Anxiety*, trans. Reidar Thomte and Albert B. Anderson, Princeton, NJ: Princeton University Press, pp. 155–62. Compare Søren Kierkegaard (1985) *Philosophical Fragments*, trans. Howard V. Hong and Edna H. Hong, Princeton, NJ: Princeton University Press, p. 83.
13 Friedrich Waismann, 'Notes on talks with Wittgenstein,' trans. M. Black, *Philosophical Review* 74:13.
14 Ludwig Wittgenstein (1958) *Philosophical Investigations*, 3rd edn, trans. G. E. M. Anscombe, New York: Macmillan Publishing Co., §499.
15 'Lecture on ethics,' p. 9.
16 Waismann, 'Notes on talks,' p. 16.
17 *Investigations*, §119.
18 *Investigations*, §373.
19 *Investigations*, §373, §371.
20 *Zettel*, §717.
21 Certainly the 'Lecture on ethics' is performing a grammatical redefinition of the concept 'ethics'!
22 *Tractatus*, §6.44; 'Lecture on ethics,' p. 11.
23 *Tractatus*, §6.45.
24 Søren Kierkegaard (1955) *On Authority and Revelation: The Book on Adler*, trans. Walter Lowrie, Princeton, NJ: Princeton University Press, p. 7.
25 *Authority and Revelation*, p. 6.

26 As one 'without authority,' Kierkegaard specifically refuses to make accusations of heresy.
27 *Authority and Revelation*, p. 13.
28 *Tractatus*, §6.421.
29 Ludwig Wittgenstein (1977) *Remarks on Colour*, trans. Linda L. McAlister and Margarete Schättle, Oxford: Basil Blackwell, §I–58.
30 *Remarks on Colour*, §III–79.
31 *Concept of Anxiety*, p. 157.
32 *Tractatus*, §6.422.
33 *Tractatus*, §6.43.
34 *Investigations*, §133.
35 *Tractatus*, §6.521.
36 Søren Kierkegaard (1983) *Fear and Trembling*, trans. Howard V. Hong and Edna H. Hong, Princeton, NJ: Princeton University Press, pp. 38–9.
37 *Fear and Trembling*, p. 36.
38 *Tractatus*, §6.521, §6.54.
39 *Investigations*, p. 227e. See also §584 (and various other references).
40 Ludwig Wittgenstein (1980) *Culture and Value*, trans. Peter Winch, Chicago, IL: University Press, p. 32e (1937).
41 *Remarks on Colour*, §III-317.
42 *Zettel*, §144.
43 *Zettel*, §141.
44 Ludwig Wittgenstein (1967) *Lectures and Conversations on Aesthetics, Psychology and Religious Belief*, ed. Cyril Barrett, Berkeley, CA: University of California Press, p. 55
45 *Zettel*, §160.
46 *Zettel*, §373.
47 *Lectures and Conversations*, p. 54; compare *Zettel*, §§378–9.
48 'Lecture on ethics,' p. 11.
49 *Lectures and Conversations*, p. 62.
50 *Lectures and Conversations*, p. 53.
51 *Culture and Value*, p. 53e (1946).
52 *Culture and Value*, p. 64e (1947).
53 The closest Wittgenstein comes to making such an appeal is: 'Go on, believe! It does no harm.' (*Culture and Value* p. 45e [*c.* 1944].) Oddly, this looks like Pascal's Wager. But the pseudo-rational choice of religion suggested by the Wager does not square with Wittgenstein's other remarks on religion or beliefs in general.
54 *Lectures and Conversations*, pp. 54–5.
55 *Journals and Papers*, §6224 (IX A 208).
56 *Journals and Papers*, §653 (VIII^2 B 85:7). See the notes on 'Reduplication,' 3:910.
57 *Journals and Papers*, §3049 (VIII^1 A 331).
58 Søren Kierkegaard (1987) *Either/Or*, 2 vols, trans. Howard V. Hong and Edna H. Hong, Princeton, NJ: Princeton University Press, 2:57.
59 Fergus Kerr (1986) *Theology after Wittgenstein*, Oxford: Basil Blackwell, pp. 28–31.

60 Waismann, 'Notes on talks,' p. 13.
61 *Journals and Papers*, §8 (X^2 A 592).
62 *Philosophical Fragments*, p. 42.
63 *Culture and Value*, p. 85e (1950).
64 *Postscript*, p. 179n. The following exchange between Norman Malcolm and Wittgenstein may throw some light on this formulation. Malcolm (quoting[?] Kierkegaard): 'How can it be that Christ does not exist, since I know that he has saved me?' Wittgenstein: 'You see! It isn't a question of *proving* anything!' (Norman Malcolm (1984) *Ludwig Wittgenstein: A Memoir*, 2nd edn. New York: Oxford University Press, p. 59) See (1941) *For Self-Examination*, trans. Walter Lowrie, Princeton, NJ: Princeton University Press, pp. 87ff, for a passage of which this might be a paraphrase. See also *Journals and Papers*, §3615 (X^4 A 210).
65 Søren Kierkegaard (1941) *Thoughts on Crucial Situations in Human Life*, trans. David F. Swenson, ed. Lillian Marvin Swenson, Minneapolis, MN: Augsburg Publishing House, p. 111.
66 *Postscript*, p. 174.
67 *Investigations*, p. 223e.
68 As has been suggested above, only a *dissolution* can be of any use in this problem.
69 *Culture and Value*, p. 86e (1950).
70 *Investigations*, p. 180e.
71 *Lectures and Conversations*, p. 54.
72 *Culture and Value*, p. 83e (1949).
73 Søren Kierkegaard (1980) *The Sickness Unto Death*, trans. Howard V. Hong and Edna H. Hong, Princeton, NJ: Princeton University Press, p. 131.
74 *Culture and Value*, p. 72e (1948).
75 *Culture and Value*, p. 80e (1949).
76 This metaphorical tension is present between language-games in general. Whenever the same word is used in varying circumstances, there will be some disanalogy, that is, some limits to the application of the metaphor implied by the use of the term. See *Investigations*, p. 188e.
77 'because the search says more than the discovery' *Zettel*, §457.
78 *Postscript*, p. 97.
79 *Investigations*, §133.
80 Of course, his ethics is in turn based on aesthetics. It might be more settling to say that his work displays recurring themes. Certainly personal responsibility is one of these.
81 In 1930, Wittgenstein remarked to M. O'C. Drury: 'For a truly religious man, nothing is tragic.' (Maurice O'C. Drury (1981) 'Conversations with Wittgenstein,' in *Ludwig Wittgenstein: Personal Recollections*, Totowa, NJ: Rowman & Littlefield, p. 122.) Cf. Kierkegaard's remarks on the difference between the religious and the tragic in *Fear and Trembling*, p. 59.
82 This is explicitly admitted by Alvin Plantinga. He remarks that theists may find evil a problem; but this is not the 'problem of evil' which might lead to disbelief or show the *logical inconsistency* of theism. 'Such a

problem calls, not for philosophical enlightenment, but for pastoral care.' See (1977) *God, Freedom, and Evil*, Grand Rapids, MI: Eerdmans, pp. 64–65. His suggestion presupposes a discouraging gulf between philosophy of religion and religion.
83 Ernest Gellner, *Cause and Meaning in the Social Sciences*, quoted in Alan Keightley (1976) *Wittgenstein, Grammar and God*, London: Epworth Press, p. 109.
84 Compare Nietzsche's idea: 'Truth is the kind of error without which a certain species of life could not live. The value for *life* is ultimately decisive.' From (1968) *The Will to Power*, trans. Walter Kaufmann and R. J. Hollingdale, New York: Vintage Books, §493.

5 ECHOES AND REPERCUSSIONS

1 Søren Kierkegaard (1941) *Concluding Unscientific Postscript*, trans. David F. Swenson and Walter Lowrie, Princeton, NJ: Princeton University Press, p. 72.
2 *Postscript*, p. 332n.
3 Søren Kierkegaard (1980) *The Concept of Anxiety*, trans. Reidar Thornte and Albert B. Anderson, Princeton, NJ: Princeton University Press, p. 142.
4 Søren Kierkegaard (1967–75) *Søren Kierkegaard's Journals and Papers*, 7 vols, ed. and trans. Howard V. Hong and Edna H. Hong, Bloomington, IN: Indiana University Press, §649 (VIII^2 B 81), ¶14.
5 Søren Kierkegaard (1948) *Purity of Heart is To Will One Thing*, trans. Douglas V. Steere, New York: Harper Torchbooks, pp. 178–82.
6 *Journals and Papers*, §6224 (IX A 208).
7 As is remarked in the notes to 'Redoubling' in the *Journals and Papers* (3:908), for Kierkegaard the ultimate expression of this reduplication is the self's synthesis in religious faith.
8 Karl Britton (1967) 'Portrait of a philosopher,' in *Ludwig Wittgenstein: The Man and His Philosophy*, ed. K. T. Fann, New York: Dell, p. 58.
9 Ludwig Wittgenstein (1947) *Culture and Value*, trans. Peter Winch, Chicago, IL: University of Chicago Press, p. 61e.
10 *Culture and Value*, pp. 61e-62e (1947).
11 Søren Kierkegaard (1987) *Either/Or*, 2 vols, trans. Howard V. Hong and Edna H. Hong, Princeton, NJ: Princeton University Press, 1:32.
12 G. E. Moore (1954–5) 'Wittgenstein's lectures in 1930–33,' *Mind* 253:26–7.
13 Søren Kierkegaard (1985) *Philosophical Fragments*, trans. Howard V. Hong and Edna H. Hong, Princeton, NJ: Princeton University Press, p. 36.
14 Moore, 'Wittgenstein's lectures,' 253:26.
15 Søren Kierkegaard (1983) *Fear and Trembling*, trans. Howard V. Hong and Edna H. Hong, Princeton, NJ: Princeton University Press, p. 123.
16 Ludwig Wittgenstein (1958) *Philosophical Investigations*, trans. G. E. M. Anscombe, New York: Macmillan Publishing Co., §133.
17 Friedrich Nietzsche, quoted in George Allen Morgan (1941) *What*

Nietzsche Means, Cambridge, MA: Harvard University Press, p. 19.
18 Nietzsche, quoted in Morgan, *What Nietzsche Means*, p. 24.
19 Further comments on this point may be found in the work of O. K. Bouwsma. See for example his (1982) 'A new sensibility,' in *Toward a New Sensibility*, ed. J. L. Craft and R. E. Hustwit, Lincoln, NE: University of Nebraska Press, pp. 1–4.
20 Maurice O'C. Drury (1981) 'Conversations with Wittgenstein' in *Ludwig Wittgenstein: Personal Recollections*, ed. Rush Rhees, Totowa, NJ: Rowman & Littlefield, p. 171. In addition to this quotation from *King Lear*, he thought of the phrase 'You'd be surprised!'
21 Søren Kierkegaard (1941) *Judge for Yourselves!*, trans. Walter Lowrie, Princeton, NJ: Princeton University Press, pp. 187–8.
22 Søren Kierkegaard (1943) *Edifying Discourses*, 4 vols, ed. and trans. Howard V. Hong and Edna H. Hong, Bloomington, IN: Indiana University Press, 4:119.
23 Kierkegaard has constantly in view another kind of 'fact' entirely: the positing of man by God. Here there may be a large difference between the two authors. The epistemological and ontological status of the 'fact' of man's dependency would be the subject for a long treatment. See chapter 4 for a brief discussion of his remark that God is 'a postulate' – a non-metaphysical fact? – for the believer.
24 Moore, 'Wittgenstein's lectures,' 249:5.
25 See chapter 3.
26 Note that for Wittgenstein, in contradistinction to some interpreters and/or borrowers of his work, 'language' is an extension of 'the deed,' rather than most 'deeds' being an extension of language – 'the language of dance,' 'the language of facial expression,' and so forth.
27 Ludwig Wittgenstein (1975) *Philosophical Remarks*, trans. Raymond Hargreaves and Roger White, Oxford: Basil Blackwell, p. 8.
28 *Postscript*, p. 178.
29 See chapter 3.
30 *Fear and Trembling*, p. 123.
31 Friedrich Nietzsche (1968) *The Will to Power*, trans. W. Kaufmann and R.J. Hollingdale, New York: Vintage Books, §481.
32 *Fragments*, p. 83.
33 Friedrich Nietzsche (1974) *The Gay Science*, trans. Walter Kaufmann, New York: Vintage Books, §299.
34 Michael Polanyi (1958) *Personal Knowledge*, Chicago, IL: The University of Chicago Press, p. 311.
35 *Investigations*, §133; emphasis added.
36 The systematic appearance of the *Tractatus* belies the personal struggle that underlay it, as well. This struggle is clearly shown in his notebooks and letters from the time when he was writing it. And it also caused headaches for those (like Russell) who tried to follow its development.
37 Ludwig Wittgenstein (1969) *On Certainty*, trans. Denis Paul and G. E. M. Anscombe, New York: Harper Torchbooks, §174.
38 Polanyi, *Personal Knowledge*, p. 315. *Commitment* looks like more than *certainty*; the word stresses the active dimension of the choice. This puts Polanyi closer to Kierkegaard (whose name does not appear in *Personal Knowledge*).

39 *Journals and Papers*, §5100 (I A 75), written August 1, 1835 – the most famous Gilleleie entry.
40 *Postscript*, p. 306.
41 *Journals and Papers*, §4550 (X^2 A 299).
42 Terence Penelhum has expressed just this frustration – that his airtight proofs in the field of natural theology should fail to convince. (For example, in his comments on George Mavrodes' paper 'The prospect for natural theology,' presented in the meeting of the Society of Christian Philosophers at the 83rd Annual Meeting of the Eastern Division of the American Philosophical Association, Boston, MA, December 27, 1986.)
43 It is astonishing that Polanyi does not make more explicit use of Wittgenstein's work, although he does mention that work briefly in *Personal Knowledge*.
44 Anthony C. Thiselton (1980) *The Two Horizons: New Testament Hermeneutics and Philosophical Description with Special Reference to Heidegger, Bultmann, Gadamer, and Wittgenstein*, Grand Rapids, MI: Eerdmans, p. 392.
45 Thiselton, *The Two Horizons*, pp. 406–7.
46 Søren Kierkegaard (1980) *The Sickness Unto Death*, trans. Howard V. Hong and Edna H. Hong, Princeton, NJ: Princeton University Press, p. 13.
47 Ludwig Wittgenstein (1974) *Tractatus Logico-Philosophicus*, trans. D. F. Pears and B. F. McGuinness, New York: The Humanities Press, §5.62.
48 *Tractatus*, §5.631.
49 *Tractatus*, §5.641.
50 *Sickness Unto Death*, p. 14.

6 NOW I CAN GO ON!

1 Maurice O'C. Drury (1981) 'Conversations,' in *Ludwig Wittgenstein: Personal Recollections*, ed. Rush Rhees, Totowa, NJ: Rowman & Littlefield, p. 124.
2 Ludwig Wittgenstein (1974) *Tractatus Logico-Philosophicus*, trans. D. F. Pears and B. F. McGuinness, New York: The Humanities Press, §5.62: '*der Sprache, die allein ich verstehe.*' In this context, arguments over the appropriate translation – 'the only language which I understand,' 'the language which I alone understand' – appear misplaced; both seem appropriate and necessary.
3 Ludwig Wittgenstein (1958) *Philosophical Investigations*, 3rd edn, trans. G. E. M. Anscombe, New York: Macmillan Publishing Co., §88.
4 Drury, 'Conversations,' p. 182.

BIBLIOGRAPHY

BIBLIOGRAPHIES

Kierkegaard

Himmelstrup, J., assisted by Birket-Smith, K. (1962) *Søren Kierkegaard; International Bibliographi*, Copenhagen: Nyt Nordisk Forlag.

Hong, H. V., Hong, E. H., and Malantschuk, G. (1967–75) Bibliographies in *Søren Kierkegaard's Journals and Papers*, 7 vols, ed. and trans. H. V. Hong and E. H. Hong, with G. Malantschuk, Bloomington, IN: Indiana University Press, 1967–75. General bibliography, 1:481–488; topical bibliographies included in notes to each subject heading.

Lapointe, F. H. (1980) *Søren Kierkegaard and His Critics: An International Bibliography of Criticism*, Westport, CT: Greenwood Press.

Wittgenstein

Fann, K. T. (1967) 'A Wittgenstein bibliography,' *International Philosophical Quarterly* 7:317–39.

—— (1969) 'Supplement to the Wittgenstein bibliography,' *Revue Internationale de Philosophie* 23:363–70.

Lapointe, F. H. (1980) *Ludwig Wittgenstein: A Comprehensive Bibliography*, Westport, CT: Greenwood Press.

PRIMARY SOURCES

Kierkegaard

Kierkegaard, S. (1971) *Christian Discourses; The Lilies of the Field and the Birds of the Air; Three Discourses at the Communion on Fridays*, trans., with introduction and notes by W. Lowrie, Princeton, NJ: Princeton University Press.

—— (1980) *The Concept of Anxiety*, ed. and trans., with introduction and notes by R. Thomte, with A. B. Anderson, Princeton, NJ: Princeton University Press.

—— (1968) *The Concept of Irony, with Constant Reference to Socrates*, trans. L. M. Capel, Bloomington, IN: Indiana University Press.
—— (1941) *Concluding Unscientific Postscript*, trans. D. F. Swenson and W. Lowrie, Princeton, NJ: Princeton University Press for the American–Scandinavian Foundation.
—— (1943) *Edifying Discourses*, 4 vols, trans. D. F. Swenson and L. M. Swenson, Minneapolis, MN: Augsburg Publishing House.
—— (1987) *Either/Or*, 2 vols, ed. and trans., with introduction and notes by H. V. Hong and E. H. Hong, Princeton, NJ: Princeton University Press.
—— (1983) *Fear and Trembling*; *Repetition*, ed. and trans., with introduction and notes by H. V. Hong and E. H. Hong, Princeton, NJ: Princeton University Press.
—— (1941) *For Self-Examination*; *Judge for Yourselves!*; *Three Discourses, 1851*, trans., with introduction and notes by W. Lowrie, Princeton, NJ: Princeton University Press.
—— (1946) *A Kierkegaard Anthology*, ed. R. Bretall, Princeton, NJ: Princeton University Press.
—— (1968) *Kierkegaard's Attack Upon 'Christendom,'* trans., with introduction by W. Lowrie; new introduction by H. A. Johnson, Princeton, NJ: Princeton University Press.
—— (1955) *On Authority and Revelation: The Book on Adler*, trans., with introduction and notes by W. Lowrie, Princeton, NJ: Princeton University Press.
—— (1985) *Philosophical Fragments*; *Johannes Climacus*, ed. and trans., with introduction and notes by H. V. Hong and E. H. Hong, Princeton, NJ: Princeton University Press.
—— (1962) *The Point of View for My Work as an Author: A Report to History*, and related writings, trans., with introduction and notes by W. Lowrie; newly ed. with preface by B. Nelson, New York: Harper Torchbooks.
—— (1962) *The Present Age*; *Of the Difference Between a Genius and an Apostle*, trans. A. Dru, introduction by W. Kaufmann, New York: Harper Torchbooks.
—— (1948) *Purity of Heart is To Will One Thing*, trans., with introductory essay by D. V. Steere, New York: Harper Torchbooks.
—— (1980) *The Sickness Unto Death*, ed. and trans., with introduction and notes by H. V. Hong and E. H. Hong, Princeton, NJ: Princeton University Press.
—— (1967–75) *Søren Kierkegaard's Journals and Papers*, 7 vols, ed. and trans. H. V. Hong and E. H. Hong, with G. Malantschuk, Bloomington, IN: Indiana University Press.
—— (1940) *Stages on Life's Way*, trans. W. Lowrie, Princeton, NJ: Princeton University Press.
—— (1941) *Thoughts on Crucial Situations in Human Life*, trans. D. F. Swenson, ed. L. M. Swenson, Minneapolis, MN: Augsburg Publishing House.
—— (1941) *Training in Christianity* and the Edifying Discourse which

'accompanied' it, trans., with introduction and notes by W. Lowrie, Princeton, NJ: Princeton University Press.
—— (1978) *Two Ages*, ed. and trans., with introduction and notes by H. V. Hong and E. H. Hong, Princeton, NJ: Princeton University Press.
—— (1962) *Works of Love*, trans. H. V. Hong and E. H. Hong, preface by R. Gregor Smith, New York: Harper Torchbooks.

Wittgenstein

Bouwsma, O. K. (1986) *Wittgenstein: Conversations 1949–1951*, ed. J. L. Craft and R. E. Hustwit, Indianapolis, IN: Hackett Publishing Co.
Engelmann, P. (1967) *Letters from Ludwig Wittgenstein, with a Memoir*, trans. L. Furtmüller, ed. with an appendix by B. F. McGuinness, Oxford: Basil Blackwell.
Waismann, F. (1965) 'Notes on talks with Wittgenstein,' trans. M. Black, *Philosophical Review* 74:12–16.
Wittgenstein, L. (1960) *The Blue and Brown Books*, 2nd edn, New York: Harper Torchbooks.
—— (1980) *Culture and Value*, ed. G. H. von Wright with H. Nyman, trans. P. Winch, Chicago, IL: University of Chicago Press.
—— (1982) *Last Writings on the Philosophy of Psychology*, vol. I, ed. G. H. von Wright and H. Nyman, trans. C. G. Luckhardt and M. A. E. Aue, Chicago, IL: University of Chicago Press.
—— (1967) *Lectures and Conversations on Aesthetics, Psychology and Religious Belief*, ed. C. Barrett, Berkeley, CA: University of California Press.
—— (1979) 'Letters to Ludwig von Ficker,' ed. A. Janik, trans. B. Gillette, in *Wittgenstein: Sources and Perspectives*, ed. C. G. Luckhardt, Ithaca, NY: Cornell University Press.
—— (1974) *Letters to Russell, Keynes and Moore*, ed. with an introduction by G. H. von Wright, with B. F. McGuinness, Ithaca, NY: Cornell University Press.
—— (1979) *Notebooks 1914–1916*, 2nd edn, ed. G. H. von Wright and G. E. M. Anscombe, trans. G. E. M. Anscombe, Chicago, IL: University of Chicago Press.
—— (1969) *On Certainty*, ed. G. E. M. Anscombe and G. H. von Wright, trans. D. Paul and G. E. M. Anscombe, New York: Harper Torchbooks.
—— (1974) *Philosophical Grammar*, ed. R. Rhees, trans. A. Kenny, Oxford: Basil Blackwell.
—— (1958) *Philosophical Investigations*, 3rd edn, trans. G. E. M. Anscombe, New York: Macmillan Publishing Co.
—— (1975) *Philosophical Remarks*, trans. R. Hargreaves and R. White, Oxford: Basil Blackwell.
—— (1977) *Remarks on Colour*, ed. G. E. M. Anscombe, trans. L. L. McAlister and M. Schättle, Oxford: Basil Blackwell.
—— (1979) *Remarks on Frazer's 'Golden Bough,'* trans. R. Rhees, Atlantic Highlands, NJ: Humanities Press.

BIBLIOGRAPHY

—— (1978) *Remarks on the Foundations of Mathematics*, rev. edn, ed. G. H. von Wright, R. Rhees, and G. E. M. Anscombe, trans. by G. E. M. Anscombe, Cambridge, MA: MIT Press.
—— (1980) *Remarks on the Philosophy of Psychology*, 2 vols, ed. G. E. M. Anscombe, G. H. von Wright, and H. Nyman, trans. G. E. M. Anscombe, C. G. Luckhardt, and M. A. E. Aue, Chicago, IL: University of Chicago Press.
—— (1974) *Tractatus Logico-Philosophicus*, the German text of Wittgenstein's *Logische-philosophische Abhandlung*, rev. edn. trans. D.F. Pears and B. F. McGuinness, with introduction by Bertrand Russell, New York: The Humanities Press.
—— (1979) *Wittgenstein and the Vienna Circle*, conversations recorded by F. Waismann, ed. B. McGuinness, trans. J. Schulte and B. McGuinness, New York: Barnes & Noble Books.
—— (1965) 'Wittgenstein's lecture on ethics,' *Philosophical Review* 74:3–12.
—— (1970) *Zettel*, ed. G. E. M. Anscombe and G. H. von Wright, trans. G. E. M. Anscombe, Berkeley, CA: University of California Press.

SECONDARY SOURCES

Kierkegaard

Allison, H. E. (1967) 'Christianity and nonsense,' *Review of Metaphysics* 20:432–60.
Bell, R. H. and Hustwit, R. E. (eds) (1978) *Essays on Kierkegaard and Wittgenstein: On Understanding the Self*, Wooster, OH: The College of Wooster.
Bonifazi, C. (1953) *Christendom Attacked: A Comparison of Kierkegaard and Nietzsche*, London: Rockliffe.
Clair, A. (1976) *Pseudonymie et Paradoxe: La Pensée Dialectique de Kierkegaard*, Paris: J. Vrin.
Gill, J. H. (ed.) (1969) *Essays on Kierkegaard*, Minneapolis, MN: Burgess Publishing Company.
Holmer P. L. (1955) 'Kierkegaard and religious propositions,' *Journal of Religion* 35:135–46.
—— (1957) 'Kierkegaard and theology,' *Union Seminary Quarterly Review* 12:3:23–31.
—— (1971) 'Indirect communication: something about the sermon,' *Perkins Journal* 24:2:14–24.
Hustwit, R. E. (1975) 'Some notes on what Kierkegaard calls "an ideal interpretation,"' *Ohio Journal of Religious Studies* 3:1:55–60.
—— (1978) 'Understanding a suggestion of Professor Cavell's: Kierkegaard's religious stage as a Wittgensteinian "form of life,"' *Philosophy Research Archives* 4:329–47.
—— (1980) 'More notes on Kierkegaard's "ideal interpretation,"' *Journal of Religious Studies* [Ohio] 8:2:12–18.
Johnson, R. H. (1972) *The Concept of Existence in the 'Concluding Unscientific Postscript'*, The Hague: Martinus Nijhoff.

BIBLIOGRAPHY

Kern, E. (1970) *Existential Thought and Fictional Technique: Kierkegaard, Sartre, Beckett*, New Haven, CT: Yale University Press, pp. 1–83, 241–3.
Lowrie, W. (1946) *A Short Life of Kierkegaard*, Princeton, NJ: Princeton University Press.
—— (1962) *Kierkegaard*, 2 vols, New York: Harper Torchbooks.
McLane, E. (1977) 'Kierkegaard and subjectivity', *International Journal for Philosophy of Religion* 4:211–32.
McKinnon, A. (1967) 'Kierkegaard': 'paradox' and 'irrationalism,' *Journal of Existentialism* (Spring).
Malantschuk, G. (1971) *Kierkegaard's Thought*, ed. and trans. H. V. Hong and E. H. Hong, Princeton, NJ: Princeton University Press.
Mourant, J. A. (1961) 'The limitations of religious existentialism,' *International Philosophical Quarterly* 1:437–52.
Sefler, G. F. (1971) 'Kierkegaard's religious truth: the three dimensions of subjectivity,' *International Journal for Philosophy of Religion* 2:43–52.
Taylor, M. C. (1975) 'Language, truth and indirect communication,' *Tijdschrift voor Filosofie* 37:74–88.
—— (1980) *Journeys to Selfhood: Hegel and Kierkegaard*, Berkeley, CA: University of California Press.
Wahl, J. (1974) *Études Kierkegaardiennes*, 4th edn, Paris: J. Vrin.

Wittgenstein

Aidun, D. (1982) 'Wittgenstein, philosophical method and aspect-seeing.' *Philosophical Investigations* 5:106–15.
Armour, L. & Faghfoury, M. (1984) 'Wittgenstein's philosophical and religious insight,' *Southern Journal of Philosophy* 22:33–48.
Barrett, W. (1979) *The Illusion of Technique*, Garden City, NY: Anchor Books.
Bartley, W. W. III (1973) *Wittgenstein*, Philadelphia, PA: J. B. Lippincott.
Bell, R. H. (1968) 'Theology as Grammar: Uses of Linguistic Philosophy for the Study of Theology with Special Reference to Ludwig Wittgenstein,' PhD. dissertation, Yale University.
—— (1974) 'Kierkegaard and Wittgenstein; two strategies for understanding theology,' *Illif Review* 31:21–34.
—— (1975) 'Theology as grammar: is God an object of understanding?' *Religious Studies* 11:307–17.
Binkley, T. (1973) *Wittgenstein's Language*, The Hague: Martinus Nijhoff.
Bouveresse, J. (1971) *La Parole Malheureuse: De l'Alchimie Linguistique à la Grammaire Philosophique*, Paris: Les Éditions de Minuit.
Burr, R. (1976) 'Wittgenstein's later language-philosophy and some issues in philosophy of mysticism,' *International Journal for Philosophy of Religion* 7:261–87.
Churchill, J. H. (1977) 'Wittgenstein and Philosophy of Religion,' PhD. dissertation, Yale University.
Copi, I. M. and Beard, R. W. (eds) (1966) *Essays on Wittgenstein's 'Tractatus,'* New York: Macmillan.
Davis, G. S. (1984) 'The Base of Design: Relativism and Rationality in Philosophy of Religion,' PhD. dissertation, Princeton University.

BIBLIOGRAPHY

D'hert, I., O. P. (1975) *Wittgenstein's Relevance for Theology*, Bern: Herbert Lang.

Edwards, J. C. (1982) *Ethics Without Philosophy: Wittgenstein and the Moral Life*, Tampa, FL: University Presses of Florida.

Engel, S. M. (1964) 'Reason, morals and philosophical irony,' *The Personalist* 45:533–55.

Fann, K. T. (ed.) (1967) *Ludwig Wittgenstein: The Man and His Philosophy*, New York: Dell.

—— (1971) *Wittgenstein's Conception of Philosophy*, Berkeley, CA: University of California Press.

Fogelin, R. J. (1976) *Wittgenstein*, London: Routledge & Kegan Paul.

Gallagher, M. P. (1968) 'Wittgenstein's admiration for Kierkegaard,' *The Month* 225:43–49.

Gill, J. H. (1964) 'Wittgenstein and religious language,' *Theology Today* 21:59–72.

Hamilton, J. R. (1979) 'What if there were a religious "form of life,"' *Philosophical Investigations* 2:1–17.

Heller, E. (1959) 'Ludwig Wittgenstein: unphilosophical notes,' *Encounter* [London] 13:3:40–8.

High, D. M. (1972) 'Belief, falsification, and Wittgenstein,' *International Journal for Philosophy of Religion* 3:240–50.

—— (1967) *Language, Persons, and Belief*, New York: Oxford University Press.

—— (1986) 'On thinking more crazily than philosophers: Wittgenstein, knowledge and religious beliefs,' *International Journal for Philosophy of Religion* 19:161–75.

—— (1981) 'Wittgenstein on doubting and groundless believing,' *Journal of the American Academy of Religion* 49:249–66.

Hilmy, S. S. (1987) *The Later Wittgenstein*, Oxford: Basil Blackwell.

Holmer, P. L. (1968) 'Wittgenstein and theology,' *Reflection* [Yale Divinity School] 65:4:1–4.

—— (1980) 'Wittgenstein: "saying" and "showing,"' *Neue Zeitschrift für Systematische Theologie und Religionsphilosophie* 22:222–35.

Hudson, W. D. (1975) *Wittgenstein and Religious Belief*, London: Macmillan.

Hunter, J. F. M. (1973) *Essays After Wittgenstein*, Toronto: University of Toronto Press.

—— (1968) 'Forms of life in Wittgenstein's *Philosophical Investigations*,' *American Philosophical Quarterly* 5:4:233–43.

—— (1985) *Understanding Wittgenstein*, Edinburgh: Edinburgh University Press.

Janik, A. and Toulmin, S. (1973) *Wittgenstein's Vienna*, New York: Simon & Schuster.

Keightley, A. W. (1976) *Wittgenstein, Grammar and God*, London: Epworth Press.

Kenny, A. (1982) 'Wittgenstein on the nature of philosophy,' in B. F. McGuinness (ed.) *Wittgenstein and His Times*, Chicago, IL: University of Chicago Press.

Kerr, F. (1986) *Theology After Wittgenstein*, Oxford: Basil Blackwell.

BIBLIOGRAPHY

Laura, R. S. (1971) 'The positivist poltergeist and some difficulties with Wittgensteinian liberation,' *International Journal for Philosophy of Religion* 2:183–90.

Lazerowitz, M. and Ambrose, A. (1984) *Essays in the Unknown Wittgenstein*, Buffalo, NY: Prometheus Books.

Lee, H. D. P. (1979) 'Wittgenstein 1929–1931,' *Philosophy* 54:211–20.

Leitner, B. (1976) *The Architecture of Ludwig Wittgenstein*, English text by D. Young, New York: New York University Press.

Lemoine, R. E. (1975) *The Anagogic Theory of Wittgenstein's 'Tractatus,'* Janua Linguarum, Series Minor, 214, The Hague: Mouton.

Lillegard, N. S. (1981) 'Understanding and believing,' PhD. dissertation, University of Nebraska, Lincoln.

McGuinness, B. F. (1966) 'The mysticism of the *Tractatus*,' *Philosophical Review*: 305–28.

Malcolm, N. (1984) *Ludwig Wittgenstein: A Memoir*, with a biographical sketch by G. H. von Wright, 2nd edn, with Wittgenstein's letters to Malcolm, New York: Oxford University Press.

—— (1986) *Nothing is Hidden: Wittgenstein's Criticism of his Early Thought*, New York: Basil Blackwell.

Moore, G. E. (1954–5) 'Wittgenstein's lectures in 1930–33,' *Mind* 63–64; nos 249:1–15, 251:289–316, 253:1–27.

Nielsen, K. (1967) 'Wittgensteinian fideism,' *Philosophy* 42:191–209.

Pears, D. (1986) *Ludwig Wittgenstein*, with new preface by the author, Cambridge, MA: Harvard University Press.

Quinn, W. S. III (1976) 'Kierkegaard and Wittgenstein: The "religious" as a "form of life,"' PhD. dissertation, Duke University.

Reese, W. L. (1978) 'Religious seeing-as,' *Religious Studies* 14:73–87.

Rhees, R. (ed.) (1981) *Ludwig Wittgenstein: Personal Recollections*, Totowa, NJ: Rowman & Littlefield.

S. (1923) 'A logical mystic,' *The Nation and the Athenaeum* [London] 4839:657–8.

Shanker, S. (ed.) (1986) *Ludwig Wittgenstein: Critical Assessments*, 4 vols, London: Croom Helm.

Sherry, P. (1972) 'Is religion a "form of life"?' *American Philosophical Quarterly* 9:2:159–67.

Thiselton, A. C. (1980) *The Two Horizons: New Testament Hermeneutics and Philosophical Description with Special Reference to Heidegger, Bultmann, Gadamer, and Wittgenstein*, with foreword by J. B. Torrance, Grand Rapids, MI: Eerdmans.

Tranøy, K. E. (1976) 'Wittgenstein in Cambridge 1949–51, some personal recollections,' in *Essays on Wittgenstein in Honor of G. H. von Wright*, Acta Philosophica Fennica 28, Amsterdam: North Holland Publishing Co.

Whittaker, J. H. (1974) '"Forms of life" and religious belief,' PhD. dissertation, Yale University.

—— (1978) 'Wittgenstein and religion: some later views of his later work,' *Religious Studies Review* 4:188–93.

—— (1983) '*Tractatus* 6.4312: immortality and the riddle of life,' *Philosophical Investigations* 6:37–48.

Zemach, E. (1964) 'Wittgenstein's philosophy of the mystical,' *Review of Metaphysics* XVIII:38–57.

RELATED WORKS

Bouwsma, O. K. (1965) *Philosophical Essays*, Lincoln, NE: University of Nebraska Press.
—— (1982) *Toward a New Sensibility: Essays of O. K. Bouwsma*, Ed. and with introduction by J. L. Craft and R. E. Hustwit, Lincoln, NE: University of Nebraska Press.
—— (1984) *Without Proof or Evidence: Essays of O. K. Bouwsma*, ed. and with introduction by J. L. Craft and R. E. Hustwit, Lincoln, NE: University of Nebraska Press.
Cavell, S. (1964) 'Existentialism and analytic philosophy,' *Daedalus* 93:946–74.
—— (1969) *Must We Mean What We Say?* New York: Charles Scribner's Sons.
Chatterjee, M. (1981) *The Language of Philosophy*, The Hague: Martinus Nijhoff.
Drury, M. O'C. (1973) *The Danger of Words*, New York: Humanities Press.
Geertz, C. (1983) *Local Knowledge: Further Essays in Interpretive Anthropology*, New York: Basic Books.
Holmer, P. L. (1978) *The Grammar of Faith*, San Francisco, CA: Harper & Row.
MacIntyre, A. (1981) *After Virtue*, Notre Dame, IN: Notre Dame Press.
Mitchell, B. (1981) *The Justification of Religious Belief*, New York: Oxford University Press.
Morgan, G. A. (1941) *What Nietzsche Means*, Cambridge, MA: Harvard University Press.
—— (1968) *The Portable Nietzsche*, selected and trans., with introduction, prefaces, and notes, by W. Kaufmann, New York: Viking Press.
—— (1968) *The Will to Power*, tran. W. Kaufmann and R. J. Hollingdale, ed. with commentary by W. Kaufmann, New York: Vintage Books.
Nietzsche, F. (1974) *The Gay Science*, trans., with commentary by W. Kaufmann, New York: Vintage Books.
Penelhum, T. (1986) Comments on George Mavrodes' paper 'The prospect for natural theology,' presented in the meeting of the Society of Christian Philosophers at the 83rd Annual Meeting of the Eastern Division of the American Philosophical Association, Boston, MA, December 27, 1986.
Phillips, D. Z. —— (1986) *Belief, Change, and Forms of Life*, Atlantic Highlands, NJ: Humanities Press.
—— (1966) *The Concept of Prayer*, New York: Schocken Books.
—— (1970) *Faith and Philosophical Enquiry*, London: Routledge & Kegan Paul.
—— (1976) *Religion Without Explanation*, Oxford: Basil Blackwell.
Polanyi, M. (1958) *Personal Knowledge*, Chicago, IL: University of Chicago Press.

BIBLIOGRAPHY

Tolstoy, L. (1960) *Lift Up Your Eyes: The Religious Writings of Leo Tolstoy*, introduction by S. R. Hopper, New York: The Julian Press.

Wallace, K. (1973) 'Nietzsche's and Wittgenstein's perspectivism,' *Southwestern Journal of Philosophy* 4:2:101–7.

Wilson, B. R. (ed.) (1979) *Rationality*, Oxford: Basil Blackwell.

INDEX

Abraham: 68, 70, 76, 78; absurd faith of, 83
Absolute Paradox: 45, 74, 102
Absolutism: 96, 122
Absurd: belief by virtue of, 65, 89; certainty, 83; and nonsense, 106
Adler, Adolph P.: 19, 25, 80, 107
Aesthetic: principle of interpretation, 28; stage, 37; works, 26, 37, 40, 64, 74, 101, 103
Aesthetics: and ethics, 9, 13, 15, 80–82, 88, 103
Anxiety: 75–76; ethical, 81–82
Application: of Kierkegaard, 52; of language, 59–60, 62; of philosophy, 29; point of, for therapies, 105, 115; of Wittgenstein, 52, 60, 67, 100; is wrong picture, 52, 54. *See also* extension
Appropriate: continuation, 108, 120, 122; explanation, 64
Appropriation: 47, 66, 71, 87, 90, 95, 114–15, 122; existential, 101, 116; process, 109–10, 135 n48; right and wrong, 99, 101, 116; subjective, 112, 113
Approximation-process: 109
Artificial intelligence: 58, 62, 133 n18
Assembling reminders: 22, 33, 42, 130 n34. *See also* methods
Audience: 4, 18, 39, 44, 70, 122; includes speaker, 104. *See also* listener, reader, speaker
Aufgehoben: 45. *See also* transcendence
Augustine: 11, 38, 93
Authority: 80. *See also* without authority
Authorships: 6, 29, 30, 35, 94, 103–4; 'essential' and 'premise', 80; and life, 21; religious, 33, 37, 73–74, 106, 107; unity of, 74

Bartley III, W. W.: 14, 124 n3, 127 n61

Becoming: 65, 75
Becoming Christian: 26–27, 37, 40, 48, 49, 67, 70, 98; Kierkegaard's problem, 1, 4, 33
Behaviorism: 57
Being: 65
Belief: Christian, scientific, and superstitious, 90–92; everyday, 76; historical, 76, 84; as mental process, 46, 54; is obedience, 87; proof not cause of, 90; systems of, 61; and understanding, 65; Wittgenstein and Christian, 84, 86; well-founded, 85, 91. *See also* faith, passion
Believers: 60–61, 90–93; religious, 85, 89
Blunder. *See* mistake
'Book on Adler': 80, 128 n69
Boundaries: conceptual, 120–21; of forms of life, 105; in language, 77–79, 113; transcending, 35, 77; and ugly ditch, 33. *See also* limits
Bouwsma, O. K.: 18, 117
Brown Book: 10

Causality: 90, 101, 102, 133 n18; nexus of, 91, 102
Center: grasping at, 108–10. *See also* concentricity
Certainty: action with, 64; against anxiety, 64, 66, 82, 83, 114; source of, 96, 111; subjective, 109, 112, 119
Christ: imitation of, 68; as thief, 106
Christendom: 31, 33, 68, 70
Christian: life, 70, 106; message, 19
Christian Discourses: 19
Christianity: as activity, 68–70, 92; appropriation of, 74, 83, 86–88, 90, 91; communication of, 83, 98; historical claims of, 84; point of, 31, 44, 46; prayer in, 106; spirit of, 80
Christians: by definition, 31, 33, 48; by earnestness, 68

152

INDEX

Color: 81, 88
Communication: of Christianity, 83, 98; existential, 98–99, 112. *See also* indirect communication
Concentricity: 88, 109, 122
Concept of Anxiety: 99, 103
Concept of Irony: 33, 43
Concepts: communication of, 119, 121; historical development of, 50; not well founded, 91; religious, 86; words and, 62
Conceptual scheme: 3, 54, 60, 115, 123
Concluding Unscientific Postscript: 16, 18, 19, 35, 64, 68, 70, 74, 98, 103, 135 n49; as parody of Hegel, 65–66; as philosophy, 37, 66–67
Conformity: of actions to words, 68, 70; objective, to truth, 114; objective, to rules, 123
Conscience: 87, 92
Consequences: of actions, 66, 82, 83; conceptual, of ethics, 82; of forms of life, 112
Context: 45, 52, 56, 60, 68, 74, 81, 84, 122; appropriate, 50, 122; of a task, 98
Conversion: 60, 61, 63, 72
Corrective: 3, 5, 6, 33, 42, 122; in Wittgenstein, 34
Culture and Value: 19, 73, 86, 95

Deeds: 67, 71; foundational, 60, 64; grammar of, 105; language as, 60, 62, 107; require doers, 34, 63–64, 134 n38; words and, 69, 136 n69, 141 n26
Definitions, incomplete: 34, 59
Depth: 43–44. *See also* grammar
Dialectic, existential: 75
Dialectical: tension, 48, 89, 117; thought, 3, 70, 71
'Diary of the Seducer': 24, 37, 50, 64
Dissolution: 54, 93–95, 120, 121. *See also* solution
Double Reflection: 28, 47
Doubt: 55–56, 60, 76; as grammatical misunderstanding, 87; inability to, 114; negation of, 112, 114
Drury, Maurice O'C.: 15, 18

Edification: 82, 99
Edifying Discourses: 22, 24, 26, 30, 37, 48, 68, 103–4
Either/Or: 17–19, 24, 26, 62, 81, 88, 100, 103, 105, 109. *See also* 'Diary of the Seducer'
Elucidations: 32, 36, 44, 71
Engelmann, Paul: 14, 16
Epistemology: 52

Error: 56; starting with, 37. *See also* mistake
Essence: 108; and grammar, 78; of religion, 78, 86, 93
Ethical, dimension of life, 34, 111–14; stage, 103; teleological suspension of, 78; willing, 82
Ethics: 15, 39, 76–82, 92, 94, 96; absolute standard of, 81, 96; and aesthetics, 9, 13, 15, 80–82, 88, 103; is conceptual, 82; consequences of, 82; free acceptance of, 95; general, 52; normative, 113; in the *Tractatus*, 41
Examples:
—Intermediate, 42, 44, 106
—Misleading, 11, 107
—Used in text: alchemy, 101–2; Alyusha Karamazov, 12; authors' lives, 26, 29; beetle in the box, 57; brothers (Matthew 21:28–31), 69; Christian cannibals, 83; chess, 63; civil law, 60; computer, 58; Copernican revolution, 59; coronation, 83; crossword, 44; devotional address, 30, 47, 99, 114; dissolving a spring, 54; drill sergeant, 99; duck-rabbit, 81; Evans-Pritchard and Leach, 61; everyday langauge, 43; games, 43; God's speech, 75; *golden helmet*, 81; *hausgewordene Logik*, 14–15, 29; hurricane, 11; Job, 68; Knight of Faith, 82; Last Judgement, 85–86; madman, 90, 110; memory, 62; mirror, 45–46; music, 62; Nuer at Oxford, 61; optical illusion, 45; railway terms, 31; showing objects, 55; sign for sale, 100; statements abusing grammar, 65; systems of measurement, 84; talking lion, 90; tapestry, 77; toothache, 54, 102; translation, 62; trisecting an angle, 102; ventriloquism, 67–68; westerner and primitive society, 60; young Hegelians, 97
—Using, 2, 5, 6, 11, 44, 45, 50, 59, 93, 106, 107
—Wittgenstein family and, 11
Existentialism, and Kierkegaard: 2
Explanations: and somewhere, 56–57, 64, 71, 76, 89; limits of, 34, 52, 58
Explication: 3, 76
Extension (of Kierkegaard and Wittgenstein): 53, 72, 98–99, 122–23; authors' position on, 98; by family resemblance, 97; in the spirit, 98, 115; requires personal involvement, 98; through reduplication, 99–100

Facts: appropriation of, 93, 95, 110–11; foundational, 87; historical, 76, 84;

153

INDEX

propositional, 61, 81; perspicuous connection of, 42, 47, 110, 120; as results, 110, 119

Faith: as action, 83, 93; and certainty, 66; everyday, 76, 111; 'how' of, 74, 114; leap of, 35, 103; as 'organ of the historical,' 87, 111; personal, 20, 74–75, 114; perspective of, 45, 95; and waxing of possibilities, 82–83. *See also* belief, passion

Family resemblance: 9, 31, 44, 86, 97, 104, 105, 133 n18

Fear and Trembling: 24, 70, 82

Ficker, Ludwig von: 14, 38, 75

Fideism: 51, 65–66, 72, 78, 83, 84, 94, 121

Finitude, problem of: 6, 44, 90

Form of life: individual, 90; and language-games, 62–63, 64; meaning of, 58–60; not metaphysical, 59, 121; religion as, 87; scope of, 60, 87–88, 105, 115, 121, 133 n30; as social, 53. *See also* language-games, worldview

Frazer, J. G.: 38, 50

Frege, Gottlob: 38

Freud, Sigmund: 50, 133 n28

Galtonian photograph: 10, 29, 36, 50, 53

Genius: 21, 26, 49, 80; and apostle, 26

God: love of, 69; as postulate, 90; proof of, 89–91, 95–96, 115; relation to, 82

Going further: 103, 110. *See also* remain standing

Going on: 44, 52, 61, 62, 86, 87, 102, 104, 108–10, 120, 123

Golden Bough: 38

Good will: 108–10, 123. *See also* spirit

Grammar: 43–46, 57, 59, 91, 92; deep and surface, 43, 44, 54–55, 57, 83, 89, 105; Gospel, 46; of love, 69; meaning of, 105, 131 n56; not metaphysical, 57; physical, 46, 105; subject/predicate, 107; theology as, 59, 73, 79, 116

Grammatical: construction, 107; distinction, 36; misunderstanding, 43, 62–63, 87; reminders, 59, 69, 70, 80; similarity, 55, 91; takes place of 'transcendental,' 79; task, 80

Grasping: 86, 87, 94; at center or periphery, 108–10, 108; of usage, 3

Happy man: 82, 83, 95. *See also* Knight of Faith

Hermeneutics: 115–16

Hilmy, S. Steven: 58

Holding fast: 85–87, 92, 103, 121. *See also* standing fast

Holmer, Paul L.: 34–37

Human being: 9, 85, 123

Humor: 42–43. *See also* jokes

Hypertext: 51

Imitation of Christ: 68

Inclosing reserve: 23–26

Indirect communication: 36, 46–50, 65, 127 n55; of art, 40; as common method, 2–4, 119; Kierkegaard's life as, 27; in Wittgenstein, 40–42. *See also* methods

Individual: 6, 29, 33, 47, 48, 52, 54, 57, 58, 63–64, 120, 121, 123; address to, 29, 52, 75, 103, 105; appropriation, 88–90, 113; biographical root of, 22, 24–25; instantiates language-games, 117; reader, 112–13; reduplication, 69–72, 116; responsible, 59, 49, 117; subjectivity, 111–17; task of, 114. *See also* methods

Infinite Resignation: 26

Intent: 59, 102; universal, 112–13

Intermediate links: 42, 44, 106

Interpretation: 63, 71, 96; biographical, 21–23, 28; of dreams and jokes, 50; of Kierkegaard and Wittgenstein, 52–54, 58–89, 63–65, 89; of phenomena, 45, 50, 81, 110, 111, 120; principle of, 52–53; of rules, 63–64; of traditions, 50, 61

Investigations: conceptual, 54, 58, 76, 82, 104, 105, 119, 120, 119–23; factual, 54, 55, 58, 76, 104, 119; historical, 61; psychological, 44, 101

Inwardness: is objectivity, 114; not properly hidden, 69, 136 n62

Irony: 27, 33, 36, 40, 42–43, 49, 68

Irrationalism: 51, 64–65, 121

Jesus, historical existence of: 84

Job: 68

Jokes: interpretation of, 50; philosophy through, 43, 131 n50

Judge for Yourselves!: 106

Judge William: 18, 81, 88

Justification, of attitude, 90; personal, 114; of use, 56, 60; of method, 70

Kerr, Fergus: 88, 131 n52

Kierkegaard, Michael (Søren's father): 22–23; reference by Wittgenstein, 17

Kierkegaard, Søren. *See also* individual works

—Biography: 'attack on Christendom,' 30, 101; autobiography, 21–22; Divine Governance, 21, 27; engagement, 24, 25; genius, 21, 26; as psychologist, 44, 106; melancholy, 22, 23, 26; mystical experience, 25–26; obligation to God, 23, 27; private

154

INDEX

nature, 21; religious concern, 28; settled life, 21; similarities with Wittgenstein, 27–29; as 'spy,' 22; theology student, 23
—Divine Governance, 21, 27, 49
—Journals, 22, 24, 25, 27, 30
—Life and literature, 21–22, 26, 27, 28; Michael Kierkegaard (father), 22–23; Regine Olsen, 22, 24, 25, 128 n72
—Pseudonyms: Constantin Constantius, 27, 128 n70; Johannes Climacus, 35, 36, 46, 65, 71, 126 n34; Vigilius Haufniensis, 99
—References by Wittgenstein, 16–20, 86, 95
Knight of Faith: 82, 88, 103, 117, 128 n72, 128 n80, 138 n69. *See also* happy man
Knowing: and being able, 42, 44, 46; factual, 108, 110, 115; grammar of, 44, 105; how and what, 99, 114; psychological reports of, 54–55
Kuhn, Thomas: 115

Language: action as test of, 68–70, 99, 117; as activity, 59, 62; bewitchment of thought by, 31; beyond, 76, 78, 79, 85; as cage, 76–78, 83, 88–89; as deed, 60, 105, 107, 141 n25; everyday, 43, 65; learning, 38; limits of, 17, 34; logic of, 40; practices of, 54, 58, 105; private, 53–58; psychological, 55, 57; of religion, 93; transcendence of, 35, 41, 71, 77–78; Wittgenstein and, 1, 2; world and, 41
Language-games: action of playing, 62–63; as activity, 62, 117, 121; not metaphysical, 59, 62, 71, 88, 94, 121; not rule-governed, 62; not systematic, 59, 93; private language and, 55–58, 63; scope of, 58–62, 67, 88, 133 n30; selection of, 96; as social, 53; transcendence in, 34–35; transition between, 63–64, 85, 113–14, 134 n39, 139 n76. *See also* form of life, worldview
Latency: 89, 92, 123, 135 n49
Leading: 37–39, 70–71
Leap of faith: 28, 35, 66, 78, 103, 114
'Lecture on Ethics': 9–10, 77–80, 85, 137 n21
Lectures and Conversations on Aesthetics, Psychology and Religious Belief: 17, 73, 91
Lessing, Gotthold E.: 33, 41, 66, 93
Life: as communication, 26, 29, 49; as despair, 105, 117; everyday, 3, 11, 43–45, 55, 56, 83, 88, 92, 99, 135 n49; fruits of, 29, 69, 70; reader's, 99, 113, 120; stream of thought and, 50, 60,

69; as task, 16–17, 28, 100, 110, 113, 117, 121; and works, 4, 6, 8, 9, 22, 24, 27–29, 74
Limits: of explanation, 52; of language, 17, 34, 66, 78, 88; not wrong, 109; of philosophy, 26, 27, 31, 34, 109; showing, 34–35; of the task, 3, 21, 31–34; of thought, 32, 67, 109; of the world, 77, 78. *See also* boundaries
Listener, appeal to, 37, 40–42, 47; role of, 99, 114. *See also* audience, reader
Logic: 76, 79, 130 n39; of language, 40; place of, 38–41; suspension of, 78
Loos, Adolph: 14, 125 n18
Love, fruits of: 69, 70
Lowrie, Walter: 18, 20–22, 26, 127 n55

MacIntyre, Alasdair: 61, 67, 70, 115, 117, 133 n30
McKinnon, Alastair: 65
Malantschuk, Gregor: 48
Malcolm, Norman: 10, 11, 15, 16, 18, 28, 43
Manifest, making: 6, 82, 87
Meaning: as activity, 60; and context, 70, 111; not consensual, 60; in subject, 90; and usage, 122–23; is use, 50, 57, 133 n16; of a word, 69–70, 84, 105, 106, 123
Mental, object: 55, 58, 102; process, 55–56, 62–63, 102, 105, 132 n7; theater, 55
Metaphor: 11, 13, 139 n76
Metaphysics: error of, 54; grammar not, 57; infinite regress of, 110; of the *Tractatus*, 38, 76
Methods: cloud intentions, 55; congruity of, 2–4, 28–29, 70–72, 97; diversity of, 39, 97, 100, 101, 103, 104; heuristic, 63, 66, 121; innovation of, 97–98; of Kierkegaard, 2–4, 25, 64–65, 74; maieutic, 25, 40, 66, 67, 71, 75, 116, 121, 130 n42, 136 n62; of masks, 104, 118; of metamorphoses, 104; not systematic, 98, 102–4; of Nietzsche, 104; of present work, 4–6; reductive, 4, 50; synoptic, 103, 105, 107; used and recommended, 3, 31, 35–37, 44, 135 n43; of Wittgenstein, 2–4, 9, 63, 101–3, 107–9, 124 n1, 128 n6. *See also* assembling reminders, indirect communication, individual, particular purpose, reduplication, suggestiveness, task
Miracles: 85, 86
Mirroring relations: 8, 16, 21, 37, 41, 76–77
Mistake: 86, 96; begin with, 37–38; category-, 76, 80, 93; incompleteness not, 34, *See also* error

INDEX

Monasticism, medieval, 68
Moore, G. E.: 38, 101, 106
Muddles: 71, 100
Mystical: 31, 73, 77, 79, 82, 88, 94; experience, 25, 26, 79, 85, 128 n70; life, 88, 93
Mysticism: 17, 26, 136 n72

Naming: of objects, 57, 59; private, 56
Nietzsche, Friedrich: 19, 104, 111, 114, 117, 139 n84
Non-believers: 60, 85, 88, 93
Nonsense, and the absurd, 65–66, 106, 110; disguised and patent, 43; *Tractatus* as, 71

Objectivity: 110, 114
Objects: as foundational concept, 91, 93; grammar and, 79, 107; seeing of, 45–46; sensations not, 54, 57, 79
Olsen, Regine: 24, 25, 33, 48, 128 n72
On Certainty: 38, 112

Pain-behavior: 54, 56, 57, 60
Paradox, essential, 110; scope of, 78–79, 88–89, 92, 121; of thought, 32, 34; transformation of, 45; uses of, 64–65, 67, 78. *See also* absolute paradox
Particular purpose: 4, 26, 33–34, 37–38; of *Tractatus*, 38–39. *See also* methods
Pascal, Blaise: 138 n53
Passion: 19, 20, 32, 86, 111–14. *See also* belief, faith
Pattern: Christ as, 68; of interpretation, 5, 21, 30, 81, 95, 122; Job as, 68
Personal involvement: 4, 5, 95, 98–99, 109, 112, 113, 123
Perspective: 28, 50, 93; of faith, 45, 67, 78, 82, 83, 95, 106; shift in, 43, 45, 82–83, 111, 115
Perspectivism: 115; not metaphysical, 111
Perspicuity: 42, 108, 109
Perspicuous presentation: 2, 42, 45, 47, 120
Philosophical Fragments: 17, 19, 37, 52, 65, 79, 103, 105, 111
Philosophical Investigations: 10, 31, 38, 44–47, 49, 51, 53–56, 59, 94, 105, 112, 130 n39; purpose of, 47, 105; and religion, 73, 77–79; style of, 39, 49, 130 n34; and the *Tractatus*, 32, 46, 79, 94, 130 n44
Philosophical Remarks: 108
Philosophy: as activity, 11, 32, 62, 92, 117; analytic, 2, 77, 105, 107; desisting from, 94, 103, 109, 110, 112; irony in, 33; limited scope of, 31–34, 39, 42–43, 75, 78, 118; linguistic, 2, 60, 107; not a doctrine, 19, 32, 34, 41, 92; not an end, 100–1, 117; not foundational, 104–5; of physical science, 115; problems of, 42, 43, 46, 75; as recursive, 36–37; of religion, 95; as sickness, 42, 105; *sub specie aeterni*, 35; synoptic, 103, 105, 107; systematic, 52, 99, 101, 104, 109. *See also* methods
'Philosophy' (academic): 9, 12, 13, 15, 31, 52, 92
Picture: 91; appeal to, 87, 107, 116; application of, 45, 107
Picture theory: 76
Point of View for My Work as an Author, The: 21, 24, 26, 35–37, 40, 73, 74, 77
Pointing: 36, 65, 89, 100; to something, 76, 87, 88
Polyani, Michael: 112, 114, 115
Polemics: 26, 27, 33, 34, 42, 46, 48, 50, 129 n9
Positivism: 69, 111; logical, 54, 57, 69, 102, 108, 112, 117, 130 n42, 132 n3, 132 n10; Wittgenstein and, 2
Private, diary, 55; language, 53–56, 60, 112; naming, 55–56
Private Language Argument: 53–58, 114; and public dimension, 60; textual limits of, 53
Problem: of the age, 33; of becoming Christian, 1, 48, 84, 99, 109; of evil, 95–96; existential, 6; of finitude, 90; particular, 33–34, 38–39, 52, 63–64, 70, 94, 95; philosophical, 42, 46, 56, 109; vanishing of, 64, 82–84, 95. *See also* task
Proof: as activity, 89–90; of eternal truths, 66; geometrical, 36, 74, 90, 102, 104; of God, 19, 41, 89–90, 95, 115; as justification of attitude, 90; seeing completeness of, 89; of the soul, 17
Propositions: analysis of (*Tractatus*), 107; clarification of, 32; as elucidations, 71; transcending, 41, 71
Protractatus: 10
Psychophysical parallelism: 58
Purity of Heart: 47, 99

'Quidam's Diary': 24

Rationality: criteria of, 61, 67; everyday, 65–66, 114
Reader: change in, 99, 106; finding, 39, 66; individual, 112–13; involved, 42, 47, 51, 98–99; of Kierkegaard, 22, 24; task of, 72, 119, 120. *See also* audience, listener
Reason: 121; limits of, 3, 78–79, 83, 102; and religion, 64–65, 76. *See also* understanding

INDEX

Reasons: not new facts, 44–46; come to an end, 58
Recursiveness: 6, 37, 122
Reduplication: in life, 87, 89, 99, 113–14, 120; in philosophy, 99, 100, 112, 113, 116; this work as, 4–5. *See also* methods
Reflection: 27, 47, 99. *See also* double reflection
Reification: 52, 53, 63
Relation, to absolute *telos* and relative ends, 92, 120, 134 n39; to God, 82, 109; self as, 116, 117
Relativising, of factual understanding, 108–9, 113, 114; of philosophy, 117, 118
Relativism: accusation of, 51, 61, 64, 72, 87–88, 121; problem of, 41, 58, 60, 64, 83, 96; of values, 41
Religion: as activity, 92; as beyond world, 78; demand for action in, 69–70; grammar of, 59, 86; and language, 77–78, 83, 85; and reason, 64–65, 76; results of, 68–70, 93; and science, 85, 86, 89, 92, 93
Religious: commitment, 62, 86, 87; conversion, 61, 63; stage, 42, 99, 103; task, 25–28
Religiousness: A, 26, 89; B, 128 n72; paradoxical, 88; spontaneous, 89
Remain standing: 103, 110, 117
Remarks, grammatical: 59, 69, 107, 113, 116
Remarks on Frazer's 'Golden Bough': 37
Reminders: 2–3, 34, 43, 59, 60, 70, 79, 80, 81, 119. *See also* suggestiveness
Repetition: 2, 24, 27, 103
Results: 4, 5, 32, 35, 93, 97, 106, 119
Riddle of life: 76, 90, 103
Rules: 59, 62–63, 67, 70, 83; following, 67, 70, 123; interpreting, 59, 63; theoretical, 108; in transition, 59
Russell, Bertrand: 9, 13, 16–17, 38

Saying: and showing, 2, 32, 34, 40, 41, 132 n3. *See also* showing
Science: 91–93, 103; communication of, 40, 42, 47; magic as, 50; physical, 108, 115; roots of, 78; social, 60–64, 115, 117; teleological status of, 110; worldview of, 85–86, 122. *See also* understanding
Secular humanism: 66–67
Seeing, active, 34; of aspects, 45–46; in context, 50; as evaluation, 81, 110; the world, 71, 116, 117
Seeing aright: 39, 41, 71, 83, 93, 117, 123
Seeing-as: 43–45, 50, 60, 62, 66, 89. *See also* latency

Self: grounded in God, 48, 91; relational, 116, 117; transcendent, 77, 117
Sensation: 43, 55–57; uncertainty about, 55
Showing: 2, 4, 6, 67, 71; in Christianity, 68–70, 79, 91; ethical and logical, 34; in philosophy, 36, 40; and saying, 2, 32, 34, 40, 41; in the *Tractatus*, 32, 40, 41, 79
Sickness: 42, 105, 131 n47
Sickness Unto Death: 48, 103, 105
Silence: 40
Simile: 36, 102; religion as failed, 77
Situation: 43–46, 67, 68, 70; existential, 35
Skepticism: 76, 84
Social, categories, 71; dimension, 54, 58, 114, 123; science, 60–64, 115, 117
Society: 53, 121
Socrates: 10, 27, 33, 49
Solipsism: 116, 117
Solution: 39, 40, 42, 45, 46, 90, 94; definitive, 5, 103. *See also* dissolution
Speaker: 4, 39, 68, 99, 104, 112. *See also* audience
Spirit: of Christianity, 80; conceptual, 122; new, of Kierkegaard and Wittgenstein, 5, 98–99, 108, 110, 115, 116; of Western science, 110, 117. *See also* good will
'Spy in a higher service': 22, 26, 27, 68
Stages of life: 64, 66, 67, 78, 88, 103, 112, 115, 121; not metaphysical, 94
Stages on Life's Way: 19, 24, 64, 66
Standing fast: 87, 92, 130 n39. *See also* holding fast
Stonborough, Margarete: 14, 15, 19
Style: appropriate, 39, 40, 42; and content, 34–39, 44, 49; of Kierkegaard and Wittgenstein, 28, 30, 130 n34; of life, 28; of philosophy, 10, 18, 50, 53, 97, 105, 118
Subject: individual, 51, 53, 54, 64, 76; experience of, 35, 40; not metaphysical, 116
Subjective: truth as, 33, 109, 114; appropriation, 87, 109, 112; thinker, 34, 45, 66, 116; interpretation, 110–11
Subjectivism: 64, 70, 111–12
Subjectivity: 54, 58, 64, 71; and objectivity, 74, 90; and subjectivism, 111–12; is truth, 114
Suggestiveness: 4, 6, 50, 59, 116; incompleteness as, 34. *See also* methods, reminders
Superstition: 91, 92
System: crystalline, 46; existential, 35, 63; religion not, 83, 93; 'stages' as, 42, 64, 66; static, 60, 62–64; *Tractatus* as, 38–39

157

INDEX

Task: 32–35, 46–50, 114–17, 119–22; biographical, 5, 8, 22, 27; of 'Book on Adler,' 80; Kierkegaard's, 4, 8, 23, 25, 27, 73, 75, 79, 80, 89, 101; life as, 16, 28, 98, 100, 116, 121; philosophical, 4, 100, 103, 116, 119; of present work, 4, 22, 27, 98, 115; Wittgenstein's 6, 8, 75, 79, 103, 109, 128 n30. *See also* methods, problem

Technique: 36, 39, 43, 44

Theodicy: 95–97

Theology: 112; extent of, 115; as grammar, 59, 73, 79; *via negativa* in, 129 n29

Theories: as facts, 119; reifying, 52–53; as results, 78, 119, 120

Therapies: 3, 42, 52, 103–5, 106, 120; application of, 105, 115

Theses: 2, 42, 47, 65

Thiselton, Anthony: 115, 116

Thomas Aquinas: 115

Through the Looking-Glass: 62, 63, 131 n50

Tractatus Logico-Philosophicus: drafting of, 10, 13, 39, 49, 130 n31, 141 n36; ethics in, 41; and later works, 20, 30–32, 34–35, 46, 77, 79–80, 94, 101–3, 116, 120, 130 n44; metaphysics of, 38, 76; as nonsense, 71, 130 n42; purpose of, 38–41, 47, 51; showing in, 32, 40, 41, 79; as system, 38–39; view of religion, 75–77, 88

Training in Christianity: 19

Transcendence: of language, 41, 71, 77; philosophical and faithful, 35

Transcendental: 76, 78, 81; 'grammatical' replaces, 79; logic and ethics are, 41

Transitions: personal, 123; problems of, 85, 89, 92, 114; stress on, 3, 42–43, 50, 64

Truth, by appropriation-process, 109; by approximation-process, 109–10; dialectical, 99; as error, 139 n84; Eternal Essential, 84, 109; of history, 41, 66; subjective, 33, 109, 114; for me, 112

Two Ages: 19

Understanding: mystical, 82; relativising of, 104, 108–11; and religion, 64–65, 70, 72, 78, 80; synoptic, 5, 42, 44–46, 81, 86, 89, 91, 95; theoretical, 3, 32, 39, 61, 67, 78, 85, 90, 93, 98–99, 104–5, 110, 113. *See also* reason

Usage: 2–3, 43, 45, 55–59, 69–70; meaning and, 122–23, 133 n16

Use: 56–58, 77, 79

Vanishing of problems: 64, 82–84, 95

Verification: 55, 57, 69, 130 n42

Waxing of the world: 82, 83, 117. *See also* perspective of faith

Well-foundedness: 66, 86, 91, 135 n49

Will: 32, 87. *See also* good will

Will to power: 111, 114

Winch, Peter: 58, 133 n30

Without authority: 6, 22, 25–27, 29, 49, 50, 80, 137 n26

Wittgenstein, Hermine: 11–14

Wittgenstein, Ludwig: *See also individual works*

—Biography: as architect, 14–15; in Cambridge, 8, 9, 13, 17, 18; classroom style, 10–11; culture, 12; episodic life, 8; exactitude, 14, 16; last words, 15–16; lifestyle, 12–13, 20; Lord's Prayer, 15; at monasteries, 13–14, 17; moral sense, 9–16, 18, 20, 29; music, 12, 62; as 'mystic,' 17; 'possibility of religion,' 15, 134 n34; private nature, 9, 21; schoolteacher, 11, 13, 14; similarities with Kierkegaard, 27–29; technical interests, 9; wartime service, 13, 16

—Direct references to Kierkegaard, 16–20, 86, 95

—Life and literature, 8, 11–16, 28, 29, 74; aphoristic nature, 8; disdain for philosophy, 9, 12; sewing jargon, 100

—Notebooks, 8, 10, 16, 22, 39, 49, 141 n36; as source for extension, 31

—Reading, 11–12, 15, 17, 19, 50, 123, 126 n41, 133 n28

—Relation of early and late periods, 30, 78, 79

—Religious concerns, 15, 19–20, 28, 74–75, 78, 94

—Wonders at the world, 26, 75, 76; ethical, 81

Works of Love: 18, 69, 70

Worldviews: relations between, 53, 85, 88, 94, 96; transitions between, 61, 111, 121. *See also* form of life, language games

Zettel: 57, 58, 73, 135 n49